PRAISE FOR *THE BUDDH.*

"Life is an adventure. Cory Mortenser. dom, and sense of accomplishment gained from keeping your heart and mind open to life's gifts."

—Rob Angel, Creator of *Pictionary*
WSJ Bestselling Author of *Game Changer*

"This book gave me the refreshment I needed; to put it more precisely, it was a short vacation from everything that I was reading and living. While reading this memoir, I went through the myriads of experiences with the author and lived the lives and places I have no connections with. It triggered some suppressed desires that I'd buried deep down in my mind and compelled those emotions that were just too surreal."

—The Lectorem & Books

"At times, *The Buddha and the Bee* feels like what would happen if Jeff Spicoli, Sean Penn's iconic anti-hero from *Fast Times at Ridgemont High* had taken up biking and set his sights on San Francisco. Dude.

"*The Buddha and the Bee* sort of turns the idea of the inspirational memoir upside down, a few obscenities here and there joined at the hip by an occasional joint and near daily rural roadside Chinese dinners and overnight stays in forgotten America's roadside motels."

—Devon Street Review

"The only thing I didn't like about this book was that it ended. It's not just for bikers. It speaks to the heart of anyone who's ever wondered if their life is going in the right direction. Every page is a reminder that life is meant to be lived, not spent wishing for something to change. At best, this book will change your life. At worst, you'll be left hoping Saturn returns for you."

—Lisa T.

"Humorously written book that proves life isn't about the destination, but about the journey and all the beauty that unfolds if you simply allow life to come to you... with some effort of course.

"This book is a page turner. I found myself lying in bed at night laughing aloud at the situations the author experienced, while biking across the country. And at the same time, distilling life lessons that we all encounter into compassionate and simple statements that reminds us that we're all human, living life and wanting to be happy and smile... even when hardships come our way."

—F. Schilling

"Cory takes the reader on a journey into the vast landscapes of the American West and into his deepest thoughts. Told from an honest, emotional, funny, self-depreciating perspective, it gives the reader pause to reflect on their own life and perhaps light a fire or at least stir some dormant embers of a quest for adventure. If you are a fan of *Blue Highways, Fear and Loathing in Las Vegas, On the Road, Into the Wild, A Walk In the Woods* or other similar tome, then you should put *The Buddha and the Bee* on your reading list."

—John H.

"This guy is crazy, someone who you don't want planning a trip for you, but who you'd probably love to have beers with or read a book by. A great storyteller with tons of asides and background info. If you have any interest in biking cross country, reading this will either convince yourself to do it or never try such a thing. Hopefully if you decide to, you'll plan it out better than he did."

—E.W. Bertram

"I was in just the right mood to read a book like this. Different from my usual fiction, mysteries, etc, *The Buddha and the Bee* is the story of Cory Mortensen, who decides to make his way by bicycle from Minnesota to California with almost no supplies, no helmet, and practically no plan. Along the way, he meets his share of characters, eats a ton of Subway Italian sandwiches and Chinese food, stays in some of the country's sleaziest motels and takes in the sights in every town he visits—like the giant stuffed polar bear—The White King in Elko, Nevada. His bike breaks down multiple times, but he finally makes it to California.

"Cory Mortensen is a true free spirit. I have never done anything like he's done and I am envious. I hope he continues to have adventures and write about them! This book was a great change of pace for me from my normal reads and I enjoyed it immensely."

—Eileen

"This book is engaging, humorous, and a great escape during a pandemic. Interesting facts and trivia about the landscape and cities Mortensen travels through are an added bonus. This book is a gift to the reader to examine our own lives and reveal our adventurous spirit!"

— Joyce E.

"Cory Mortensen writes about his journey biking from Minnesota to California. I 'oh, no'ed' every time a car pulled up. And, I had a mini-anxiety response every time he blew out a tyre! What really caught my attention were the historical aspects of the towns he went through. Interesting, engaging, entertaining! Well written and witty."

—Angie

BOOKS BY CORY MORTENSEN

The Buddha and the Bee:
Biking through America's Forgotten Roadways
on an Accidental Journey of Discovery

Unlost:
Roaming through South America on a Spontaneous Journey

THE BUDDHA AND THE BEE

BIKING THROUGH AMERICA'S FORGOTTEN ROADWAYS
ON AN ACCIDENTAL JOURNEY OF DISCOVERY

CORY MORTENSEN

Published by White Condor LLC

www.White-Condor.com

Hardcover: 978-1-7354981-1-9
Paperback: 978-1-7354981-2-6
Kindle: 978-1-7354981-3-3
EPUB: 978-1-7354981-4-0

Library of Congress Control Number: 2020914436

Publishing and Production by Concierge Marketing Inc.

Printed in the United States of America

10 9 8 7 6 5 4 3

This book is dedicated to:
Saturn—for returning

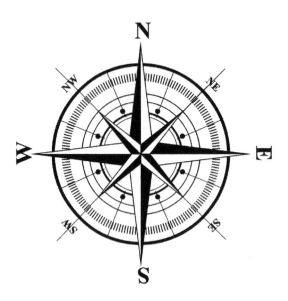

CONTENTS

"As a bee gathering nectar does not harm or disturb the color and fragrance of the flower; so do the wise move through the world."
—GAUTAMA BUDDHA

AUTHOR'S NOTE

What you are about to read is based on actual occurrences. The dates, route, meals, and consumption are all true.

The speeds at which I claim to pedal may be slightly exaggerated in an effort to impress you, the reader.

The number of flat tyres I claimed to have had, I'd put at a solid 98% accuracy.

I have changed the names of those I actually know to avoid having to share any of the profits I make from this book with them. I have made up names for those I don't know or whose names I don't remember.

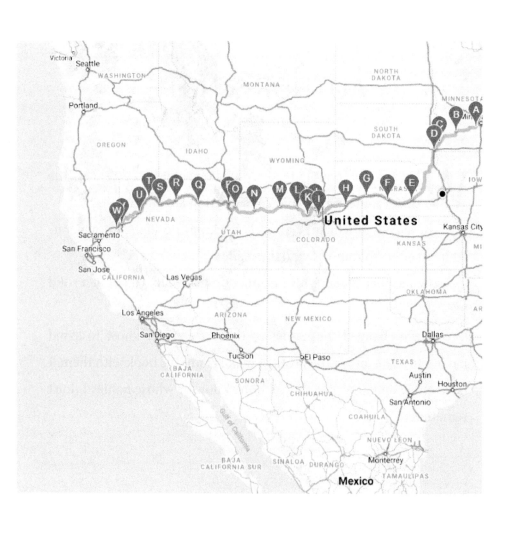

DAILY ROUTE

A > CHASKA, MN

B > REDWOOD FALLS, MN

C > PIPESTONE, MN

D > SIOUX FALLS, SD

E > GRAND ISLAND, NE

F > GOTHENBURG, NE

G > OGALLALA, NE

H > STERLING, CO

I > BOULDER, CO

J > ESTES PARK, CO

K > HOT SULPHUR SPRINGS, CO

L > STEAMBOAT SPRINGS, CO

M > MAYBELL, CO

N > ROOSEVELT, UT

O > HEBER CITY, UT

P > SALT LAKE CITY, UT

Q > WEST WENDOVER, NV

R > ELKO, NV

S > BATTLE MOUNTAIN, NV

T > WINNEMUCCA, NV

U > LOVELOCK, NV

V > RENO, NV

W > TRUCKEE, CA

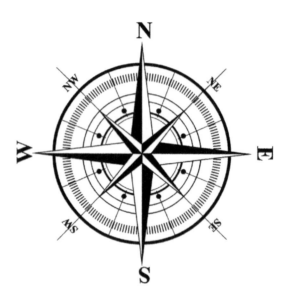

THIS IS HOW IT ENDS

The bridge offered nothing in the way of a shoulder, aside from a five-inch gap between the solid white line and the concrete wall. On the other side of the concrete wall was a fifty-foot drop into the Truckee River.

The road was clear behind me, so I started across, unaware of what the next few moments had in store for me.

Halfway across the bridge, the sound of semitrucks rumbled up behind me. I looked back and—with what could only be described as a feeling of pure terror—saw two Peterbilts closing in on me. Side by side, no room for either truck to change course.

I guessed it would take my friends and family a week to place a ghost bike[1] at this location to commemorate my final stand.

39°22'05.9"N 120°06'54.1"W

I considered jumping over the bridge into the shallow Truckee River below. But as the saying went, it wasn't the fall that would kill

---

1   A bicycle painted all white and placed at the location where a cyclist was killed by a vehicle.

you, it was the landing. I couldn't bring myself to leap, and I doubted I would survive the fall…err, landing.

A loud, long belch of horns echoed around me. Jumping wasn't an option. I turned my attention to the end of the bridge and pedaled as fast and hard as I could. The two broken spokes and the weight of my gear caused the bike to wobble viciously from side to side.

Only ten feet to go, I looked back and could see the hula dancer on the dashboard of the semi in the right lane—another long belch of the horn followed. In what I expected were my final moments, life was now moving in slow motion. As if this nightmare couldn't get any worse, two metal drainage grates found themselves right in my path. I couldn't go around them, I couldn't ride over them as the openings would have sucked in my front wheel and sent me head over tea kettle.

Just ten feet beyond the grates was the end of the bridge. I looked back again. The trucks were halfway across, just one hundred feet behind me, neither slowing down, both fighting for pole position. Another belch from the horn shattered my final nerve. I jumped off my bike, lifted it over my shoulder, and ran as fast as I possibly could.

MINNESOTA

"Sky-Tinted Water"

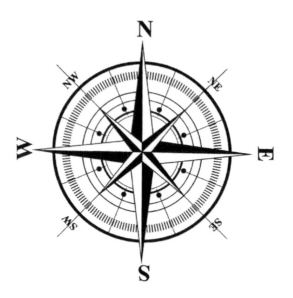

CHAPTER 1

DAY ONE

AUGUST 22, 2001

Today's Ride: Chaska, Minnesota - Redwood Falls, Minnesota
Today's Distance: 98 Miles

It was just before six a.m. and the sun was working its way toward the horizon. Your hero stood in the living room of his dad's house in Chaska, Minnesota, sipping his coffee and staring westward, out along the low-hanging trail of clouds snaking along the Minnesota River Valley.

The house sat atop a nameless bluff, surrounded by a carefully designed community with street names that let you know, without any doubt, you were, in fact, atop a bluff—Bluff Pass, Bluff Trail, Ridge Bluff Drive, Bluff Pointe Drive.

I was running one hour behind the time I had originally planned to leave. I didn't know how long it would take me to get to Redwood Falls, but I wanted to give myself as much daylight as possible. Sunset this far north at this time of year was 8:00 p.m. That gave me fourteen hours.

It was only one hundred miles to Redwood Falls. While it was true I'd never ridden that far in one day in my entire life, I didn't think it was anything I needed to be concerned about. Even at ten miles per hour, I would arrive in time for dinner. Probably still have time to squeeze in a run before the sun set.

My route wasn't exactly set in stone. It wasn't well planned out either. I spent all of about thirty minutes looking at maps and making some assumptions. I felt comfortable that there were just enough roads between me and Truckee, California, two thousand miles away.

Not only was I doing this alone with no planned route, but I also didn't even have a hotel booked for Redwood Falls. Hell, I didn't even know if Redwood Falls had hotels. I'd never been there. For the most part, everywhere I'd go over the next sixty days was going to be personally uncharted territory.

I had not locked in on which lines I would take on the seven Rand McNally maps I acquired at the AAA office. All I knew was that I had 2.6 million miles of road at my disposal and sixty days to figure it out.

Originally, the plan was to leave my house in Northeast Minneapolis at 5:00 a.m. The Cedar Lake LRT Regional Trail, which was a few blocks from my house, connected with the Minnesota River Bluffs LRT Regional Trail—a distance of twenty-four miles from my house to my dad's.

It wasn't that the ride from my house to Chaska would have been difficult, but I had had some last-minute items to pick up. Plus, my dad had offered to drive me around and take me to lunch.

Seeing no point in refusing a free lunch and saving him from having to drive me back to my house, I had decided to stay at his place for the night. The perks likely included air conditioning, cable TV, a nice dinner, and a glass or two of Jameson.

Our first stop was a local bike shop. I didn't need much—it was only two thousand miles, and the bike was almost brand new with just a few hundred miles on the odometer.

It didn't occur to me to ask the guy at the shop what he might recommend I bring on such an adventure. No, I made the executive decision that four tubes and a bike pump would be all I would need in the off chance I were to get a flat tyre[2] between Chaska and California.

After dropping forty-three dollars at the bike shop, we headed straight for Bunny's in St. Louis Park for lunch.

Bunny's was a not-so-fancy bar and restaurant where Dad and I had lunch on occasion, as it was a half-way point between our houses. He ordered the spaghetti and meatballs. We could be at Ruth's Chris Steak House, and he'd order spaghetti and meatballs. I opted for the half-pound burger and fries, rare as legally possible, with two sides of mayonnaise.

I could tell my dad had his reservations about me biking to California alone. I had zero interest in talking about the trip, but then the questions started.

"Do you have your route planned out?"

Some people just needed a destination. I never liked planning; I always end up disappointed.

---

2 Tyre is the British spelling of the word 'tire,' and how I prefer to spell it to annoy my good friend Kevin who rebuts with a link to the "Siege of Tyre" where Alexander the Great defeated the Persians in 332 BC.

"Hmm, not really. I think I'll just go west and south. Make it up as I go. Stay on the back roads."

My dad didn't always agree with how I did things, but he never let on. Up until he passed in 2009, I always knew he had my back, even though I was also pretty aware of the fact that he didn't approve of my lackadaisical approach to life.

The trip didn't sit well with him, but he wasn't going to try to persuade me not to do something I wanted to do.

◉

The first time I generated heart-stopping fear in my dad, I was a kid, probably seven or eight, sitting in the front seat of his Pontiac Bonneville. This was in the seventies, when kids could sit in the front seat and seat belts were optional. I wondered, as he was turning into a curve on I-17 just north of Phoenix, what would happen if I opened the fifteen-pound door. The centrifugal force flung the door open. I would have been thrown out of the car had it not been for his fast response. He reached over, grabbed me with his right hand while my legs dangled out of the car, and somehow managed to keep the car on the road as he slowed down and pulled me back in. He then very calmly asked me to close the door and lock it. "Don't touch the handle while I'm driving, please."

The second time was a couple of weeks after my junior year of high school. My neighbor Mary called me on a Saturday morning.

"You want to skydive with me?"

"When?" I asked.

"Right now, I'll pick you up. It's seventy-five bucks."

"Okay, I'll see you in ten minutes." I turned to my parents.

"Mary is picking me up. We're going to go skydiving. Be back by lunch."

There was silence, then my dad asked, in his calm voice, "Why do you want to jump out of a perfectly fine airplane?"

Mary picked me up, and just as we were wrapping up the fifteen-minute training and signing death waivers, I saw my dad pull up. He didn't say a word. I waved at him and boarded the tiny Cessna 182 with the three other jumpers, my tandem lead, and the pilot.

I was terrified of heights. Had it not been for the fact that Mary had already jumped, I would have willingly returned to the ground with the pilot with no refund.

Instead, we reached ten thousand feet, and the three other jumpers leaped at one time. The loss of 450 pounds sent the plane soaring up to eleven thousand feet.

If memory serves me correctly, I do believe I pissed myself a little.

The jump turned out to be a success. Dad captured the landing on VHS.

He was a pilot, a 747 captain. He worked off a checklist. People's lives depended on his experience and full understanding of procedure, processes, well-established routes, vector coordinates, squawk codes, and most importantly, staying calm under pressure. Flying by the seat of his pants was something that happened only in extreme situations, whereas my whole life was jumping into waters without checking the depth first.

I was notorious for disappearing for a week or two, whether it was a last-minute motorcycle ride cross-country, wandering around Central America, or turning a four-hour stroll to test out a new backpack into a three-day hitchhiking adventure.

Dipping my fries into some mayonnaise, I listened as my dad continued the questioning.

"Will you be carrying a gun?"

"Uh, no Dad. I don't have a gun."

"You don't have a gun!? Do you want to carry mine? I have a nice 9mm."

"I don't think I'm allowed to carry a gun across state lines."

He knew that to be true, but he was the kind of guy who would make friends with the cop even after finding a pistol on a cross-country bike ride. They would spend the afternoon shooting targets, then enjoy a beer, talking about how frustrated their oldest sons made them.

As a kid, I got caught shoplifting, not by the store, but by my dad. He took me to each store I had stolen something from—gum, candy, Legos, and beer, though I never told him about the beer. He made me apologize to all the store owners then dragged me down to the Scottsdale Police Department, where I was made to confess my crimes to a detective.

After the interrogation, the detective took me to booking and told me if I was just a couple of years older, I would be getting fingerprinted. Then he showed me the jail cell in a continued effort to scare me straight.

While I sat there crying, the detective and my dad made plans to grab a beer together later that night.

Dad's current questioning continued between bites of his spaghetti, "How will you protect yourself?"

"I don't think it will come to that. I'm pretty sure I'll be okay."

"Do you have a cell phone?"

"Nope. But I can use the internet for free at public libraries, so I'll email you when I can."

"Well, if you need help, just call me collect, and I will come get you."

"I know."

◉

I finished my coffee and walked back to my dad's spare room. I pulled on my black Lycra biking shorts and grabbed my red short-sleeved cycling jersey, pulling it down over my head. Both items were a bit snugger than I remembered, but not too unexpected after yesterday's half-pound burger.

I searched for my blue bandana and found it wedged between the pillows. I tied it around my head and strapped on my helmet.

From the refrigerator, I grabbed two sixteen-ounce water bottles. I didn't think I'd need more than two. There would be 7-Eleven's,

Circle K's, and other regional convenience stores to supply me with all the Gatorade, water, and burritos I required.

I walked through the laundry room and into the garage, which smelled of oil, bagged mulch, and fertilizer. Reaching to the left, I pressed a button to open the garage door. It was already warm and condensation from the water bottles began to drip on the garage floor.

To my right, parked in the third stall, was a John Deere riding mower. Leaning against that was my 1998 Specialized Allez. Blue with a grey stripe along the top tube for effect.

Purchased and used only once in competition in 1999, the bike was in almost perfect condition. So much so that I didn't even bother taking it to a mechanic to give it a quick look over. A couple of drops of oil on the chain and I was ready to rock and roll.

The aforementioned competition was the Minnesota Border To Border. It was a four-day race that started in the town of Luverne, located in the southwest corner of Minnesota, and ended at Crane Lake, near the Canadian border. Day one was a two-hundred-mile bike race divided equally between our three-person team. Day two was another two hundred miles of cycling, day three a fifty-mile run, and day four a fifty-mile canoe.

After the race, the bike sat dormant for two years, until one day, when cleaning my garage, I thought about how awesome it would be to go on a long bike ride. I took it out for a few ten-mile rides, and with that, I was convinced I was ready to pedal west.

It was a picture I saw once in *Outside Magazine*. The image was of a long, straight, two-lane back road that disappeared into the mountains straight ahead. I was convinced it was probably taken somewhere in Idaho or western Montana. The sky was winter grey and, in the middle of this empty and seemingly never-ending ribbon of asphalt, was a guy on a mountain bike wearing a full-sized backpack.

That image stuck in my mind for years. During one of my planning sessions at the King of Clubs in Northeast Minneapolis—made famous for its role in the movie *Fargo*—and accompanied by a few three-finger pours of Jameson, I told myself, *I too will ride my bike down a never-ending ribbon of asphalt wearing a backpack.*

Did it ever occur to me that maybe, just maybe, this guy and some buddies drove out to some long and empty road, staged the photo, sent it into *Outside Magazine*, and went back to the lodge for a few beers? Not in a million years.

When I bought the Allez, I had the option of a two-ring or three-ring crankset.[3] I opted for the three-ring without hesitation. Who in their right mind wanted to work that hard when the option of granny gear was available?

The smallest ring on a crankset was referred to as granny gear because it allowed you to pedal faster with less resistance, making climbing easier, albeit you moved forward much slower. There were eleven distinct gear ratios:

---

3   The part of the bicycle drivetrain that drives the rear wheel from the rotation of the rider's legs.

Front Ring		Rear Ring
28t	+	28t Easiest
28t	+	24t
38t	+	28t
38t	+	24t
38t	+	20t
38t	+	17t
38t	+	15t
38t	+	13t
38t	+	12t
48t	+	13t
48t	+	12t Hardest

Triple   Compact   Double

The 't' stood for teeth. The number of teeth defined the size of the chain ring.

The confusion lay with the pedaling difficulty. The smaller the front chainring and the larger the rear chainring, the easier it was. So, it would be true to say that the larger the front chainring and the smaller the rear chainring, the harder it was to pedal.

It might be fair to say that no self-respecting roadie would ever have a granny gear on his or her road bike.

A roadie had commonly been known as a cocktail or beer you bring with you on a road trip. However, in the cycling community, a roadie was a cyclist who rides road bikes. Roadies could be found in groups hanging around coffee shops on Sunday morning, sipping espressos after a fifty-mile ride. They had shaved legs, wore matching tight, color-coordinated Lycra "kits" displaying their local team colors, a recently completed event such as an MS150, or their favorite professional team, and had a full understanding of the metric system.

I wasn't a roadie. I came from the mountain bike world and having three rings on your crankset was par for the course. Mountain bikers were found drinking and eating pizza after a race, typically unwashed.

I had added a luggage rack to the back of the Allez the night before. The rack was made of aluminum and attached to the seat post with the use of a quick-release clamp, which was great, as it didn't require a lot of mechanical prowess or tools and could easily be removed in a matter of seconds.

What wasn't so great was there was no lateral support. I would later experience the downsides of this, but as I was leaving Chaska, it was an issue I didn't even know existed.

Of course, the ideal setup would have been panniers, but this bike frame wasn't designed to attach panniers. It was a race bike, not a touring bike.

On the luggage rack, strapped on with the use of two blue bungee cords, I had a tent and my sleeping bag.

I checked the tyre pressure with my newly acquired Topeak bike pump. The front and back both checked in at 95 psi. I checked the brakes by squeezing the levers, more of a delay tactic than a real brake check. Either way, they seemed to work properly.

Sliding the water bottles into the cages, I readjusted the tent and sleeping bag along with the rack.

I threw on my backpack. It weighed forty-two pounds.

"The journey of a thousand miles begins with one step," said Lao Tzu.

In my case, the journey was two thousand miles and would begin with a pedal stroke.

I was certain one hundred years from now that students would learn about my epic trip, study it, and perhaps even sing songs about it. Livingston, Earhart, Shackleton... Mortensen.

I coasted down the driveway attempting and re-attempting to clip my shoes into the pedals, looking down while doing so. I decided to wear my road cycling shoes, which would prove to be a bad idea.

Once I was clipped in, I looked up, at which point my backpack knocked my helmet down in front of my eyes. I was having my first issue and I was still in the driveway. I had to either ditch my pack or my helmet. Since everything I needed, or thought I needed, was in my pack and since it was just a helmet—nothing more than a thin plastic mold covering pressed Styrofoam strapped to my head, the purpose of which was to save my life if I were to crash and land on my head—I threw my helmet in the garage. Without a second thought, I headed out.

Now reader, before you judge me on the decision to ride two thousand miles helmetless, helmets were not mandatory for road cycling in 2001. The Tour de France didn't require helmets be worn until 2003. There, that's my justification. Now, had I done this ride in 2003 without a helmet, that would have been stupid.

I took a left out of the driveway onto Bluff Pointe Drive, then a right onto Ridge Bluff Drive, another left onto Bluff Trail, and then a left onto County Road 42.

Forty-two, I smirked, *the Answer to the Ultimate Question of Life, The Universe, and Everything.*[4] In just eight minutes, I was already closing in on California. Only 1,998 miles to go.

County Road 42 connected with US Highway 212.

The rolling hills led me out of the bluffs and into the farmland. A light fog cooled the air. It wasn't long before the sun melted the clouds away, and it very quickly became hot and humid.

August 22 was a bit late in the season to head out. My only hope was that I would have good, warm weather for as long as possible. Actually I didn't think much about the weather. I seriously assumed sunshine and lollipops, rainbows and eighty-degree temps every day. Why should I have expected anything else?

After an hour and a half of riding, I stopped in Norwood Young America, which seemed like an epic achievement in and of itself. I had gone twenty-three miles, the longest I had ridden in years. But I

---

4 In the book *The Hitchhiker's Guide to the Galaxy*, by Douglas Adams, we learn that after 7.5 million years of calculating, the supercomputer *'Deep Thought'* concludes the answer to the Ultimate Question of Life, the Universe and Everything is…4 2.

remained calm. Didn't want to brag to all those people pumping gas. They wouldn't understand the achievement.

Norwood Young America offered a couple of gas stations and houses at affordable prices still within commuting distance of Minneapolis. I wouldn't put it down on my list of places to visit unless, of course, you were one who appreciated German heritage.

Norwood Young America hosted Stiftungsfest. The dream that turned into reality was now the oldest festival in Minnesota.

In 1862, Karl Bachmann literally woke from a dream where he saw himself leading a group of men singing German songs from the nineteenth century. He jumped out of bed and found five of the best male singers he knew:

- Heinrich Bachmann

- Adolph Hoftermann

- A. Schrimpf

- H. Verufen

- Henry Hostermann

With Karl as the leader, they became known as the Pioneer Maennerchor,[5] and Karl's dream became reality.

My dream to pedal to California wasn't as grand as Karl's. The fact was, the whole idea was less of a dream, more of an idea that emerged from one too many Jamesons and a break-up.

With twenty-three miles behind me, I sat thinking about what lay ahead. The Great Plains, Rocky Mountains, an alkaline desert, and lastly, ascending the Sierra Nevadas. Seemed simple enough.

---

5   Men's choir in German.

I focused my attention on buying a Gatorade, then sat on the curb outside the Super America to study my map of the state of Minnesota. Perhaps if I looked again, closer and with greater attention, I would find a shorter way to Redwood Falls.

Instead, I found a system of perfect grids, dividing up the state and the Minnesota River—a tributary of the Mississippi River—slicing through the thousands of acres of agriculture.

Starting just south of the Laurentian Divide[6] in Big Stone Lake at the South Dakota border, the Minnesota River traveled 335 miles southeast to Mankato, then took a hard left, heading northeast up toward Minneapolis, where it connected and doubled the width of the Mississippi—as the Ojibwa called it, the Misi-ziibi, "Great River."

I finished my Gatorade and put on my pack. The weight caused me to stumble a bit. The pack seemed heavier than before. My shoulders grumbled as I straddled the top tube and looked west. The sun was at my back. Roughly seventy miles stood between me and Redwood Falls.

Eleven miles down Highway 212, I reached Glencoe.

Glen Coe, Scotland, for which Martin McLeod named this Minnesota town, was a volcanic region in the Scottish Highlands. There, the MacDonald clan was massacred in February 1692 because they would not pledge allegiance to the British crown. Glencoe, Minnesota, was a prairie town of five thousand perfectly

---

6   A continental divide in central North America that separates the Hudson Bay watershed from the Gulf of Mexico watershed.

fine Midwesterners. The most exciting thing that ever happened here was when the railway arrived in 1872.

It was rumored the Scots hitched a ride with the Vikings and arrived in North America around 985 AD. So, it wouldn't be surprising if a few of them followed the Vikings into Minnesota. In addition to the state's professional football team, the Minnesota Vikings, the belief that Vikings once roamed the land has been supported by Olof Ohman's controversial Kensington Runestone.[7] If real, the stone would prove that the Vikings were sipping lattes and journaling on stones as far back as 1362 in modern-day Minnesota.

I pressed on to Stewart and stopped at an old gas station. Its two tired, old, rusted red-and-white Bowser fuel pumps stood unprotected and unused on a crumbling concrete island. The building was a small, faded, wooden structure no more than three hundred square feet in size, including one bathroom, accessible only from the outside.

When I pulled up, my cycle computer showed I had completed fifty-two miles. My chest swelled with pride, but there was no one to share the accomplishment with. So, I sauntered into the station in search of someone anxious to hear about my achievement.

Inside the station, I found a nice selection of cold beverages, single-serving bags of chips, and plenty of Hostess products. Three men in their seventies sat at a square folding table covered with that day's newspaper, a deck of cards, and an ashtray full of butts.

---

7   A stone found in 1898 in a farm field in Solem, Minnesota, that was said to prove that the Vikings were in the United States well before Columbus. Many believe it's a hoax while others swear to its authenticity.

I grabbed a Gatorade and a package of Hostess Donettes—chocolate—and placed my selections on the counter.

On a side note: Let me clear up a misconception about Minnesota. It is assumed that Minnesota is cold. Just mention the name and people shiver. The state conjures up images of piles of deep snow, Sorels, ice festivals, down coats, toques… a child's tongue stuck to a frozen post after a triple dog dare.

It is true, winters in Minnesota are without a doubt miserable—weeks of grey skies, virtually no sun and single-digit to sub-zero temperatures. The state boasts a record low, with windchill, of -60°F. The average temperature at the North Pole in the winter is -40°F.

Turn the dial ahead six months and summers in Minnesota have a recorded high of 114°F. A temperature swing of 174 degrees. On this day, August 22, 2001, we reached 85°F, with plenty of humidity for everyone.

"Looks like you're biking," one of them said without moving his eyes from the newspaper.

"Where are you coming from then?" the cashier asked, while punching in the numbers on the cash machine.

"Started in Minneapolis," I said, with a bit of *pretty impressive, isn't it* in my voice.

"Minneapolis! You bike all this way from Minneapolis? Well, son, how far you headed then?"

"Heading to California."

"Well, okay then, Mr. California. You be safe."

With that, the conversation was over. I grabbed my change, Gatorade, and my partially melted package of chocolate Hostess Donettes, and sat out on the curb next to my bike.

Reviewing the map, I still found no shortcuts.

Just after Stewart, Highway 212 changed from a divided four-lane road to a single lane. The shoulder, noticeably wider now, included a twelve-inch-wide rumble strip used to alert drivers who might find themselves drifting off or distracted while looking for radio reception on their factory-installed Delco.

Aside from the rumble strip, only the occasional dead animal became an obstacle. In these parts, roadkill typically consisted of deer, skunk, or raccoon.

Other obstacles, which provided far less of a smell, were the dried chunks of mud and random agricultural waste that had fallen off a tractor, truck, or combine.

Traffic dwindled down to a car every ten minutes, and all I could hear were the crickets. It seemed surreal. I felt like only minutes before I was surrounded by the city, cars, pedestrian traffic, homeless folks hitting me up for spare change. Now, literal crickets.

I stopped to consider for a moment where I was. The corn was well above my head, but I could see the fields disappear as they ebbed and flowed into the horizon, silently swaying. Born into this world just seventy days ago, soon it would be harvested—food and fuel for millions of people all over the world. What had I done over the past seventy days that was of any importance?

Minnesota was responsible for 4% of the agriculture in the United States. There I was in the middle of it—me, a symphony of crickets, and the occasional passing vehicle. Pretty quiet, pretty lonely. Surrounded by all this life, it still felt so empty.

After Buffalo Lake, I decided to mix it up a bit. Well, as much as anyone could mix it up whilst riding in a massive grid of corn, soybeans, and hay. I turned south on County Road 8 for a few miles, then west onto 750th Avenue, then south again onto State Highway 4.

None of these roads really meant anything, but like the prisoner pacing his cell, counting out his steps, the roads—and their names, numbers, and distances—kept my mind on something. Anything to break the lonely monotony of empty Minnesota farmland. They allowed me to focus on math and time. By working out speed and distance, I was able to calculate and re-calculate my expected arrival at the next empty town.

Twenty miles on, I turned west on State Highway 19 and stopped in Fairfax. Maynard's Grocery Store sat a half block off Main on Park Street. I was the only traffic in town.

There were three aisles in the grocery store, fortunately offering more than I needed. I grabbed an apple, banana, and bottle of Gatorade, and placed them on the counter.

The cashier, somewhere in her late fifties, sported a heavy dose of blue eye shadow, eight Black Hills Gold rings, and the overpowering scent of perfume trying to mask the lingering smell of cigarette smoke. She smiled, smacked her gum, and scanned the Gatorade.

"Sure is hot." Without giving me time to respond, she followed up with, "That's $4.23. You want a bag then?"

"No bag." I handed her a five.

With change, apple, banana, and Gatorade in hand, I headed back outside, grabbed my bike, and walked it across the street to Memorial Park to eat and rest.

Seventy-eight miles behind me, I thought I was doing pretty good. Of course, I had nothing to base that on. Seventy-eight miles in seven hours, including stops. My average speed was about twelve miles per hour. My body was feeling a bit beat up, between the backpack, bike saddle, and fresh sunburn. I had to keep pedaling forward though, no time yet to rest and recover.

To look at Fairfax, you might assume that nothing had ever happened there. As I sat in Memorial Park, I wouldn't have disagreed with you. Eben Ryder had arrived 111 years earlier from Virginia, naming the place after his hometown. The town had grown an average of 8.41 people per year, proudly harboring a current population of 1,285. Plus, one cyclist.

Just a few miles south of Fairfax was Fort Ridgely, built in 1853. It was the location of two battles during the Dakota War of 1862, also referred to as the Sioux Uprising. The war only lasted a few months, but it led to the capture of thousands of Sioux, of which more than three hundred were tried and sentenced to death for treason. In the end, President Abe Lincoln whittled that number down to thirty-eight. December 26, 1862, those unlucky thirty-eight were hung on a single platform in what is still to this day the largest mass execution by the government in US American history.

Following the execution, the bodies of the executed Sioux were stolen, likely sold to doctors for research, as was common practice. The body of Marpiya te najin—He Who Stands in the Clouds—was dug up from the mass grave of the thirty-eight by William Worrall Mayo for study. His son would later found the world renowned Mayo Clinic. Mayo dissected the body, dried and varnished the skeleton, and hung it in the front room of the clinic. In 1998, the Mayo Clinic finally returned the remains to the Sioux for reburial per the Native American Graves Protection and Repatriation Act, and the Mayo Clinic symbolically apologized by creating the Marpiya te najin Scholarship.

One hundred and thirty-nine years later, near this former battlefield where the Dakota were defeated, I ate my banana and took a fifteen-minute nap on a picnic table.

Back on my bike and heading west on SH 19, I passed a sign that read: *Redwood Falls 21 mi.*

Beginning in Fairfax, the Twin Cities and Western Railroad (TCWR) ran parallel with SH 19. The tracks followed me straight into Redwood Falls. Originally built in the late nineteenth century by the Minneapolis and St. Louis Railway, the TCWR started in Norwood Young America and ended in Granite Falls, transporting corn, soybeans, fertilizers, ethanol, butter, lumber, canned vegetables, biodiesel, tallow, salt, and aggregates.

The next town, just eight miles west, was Franklin—named after Benjamin Franklin and home to five hundred people... and Catfish Derby Days. Five miles after Franklin, I reached Morton. The town offered up an Amstar gas station, which I chose to skip, continuing directly onto Redwood Falls. I could see the finish line and I desperately wanted to be there.

These towns, little though they were, were instrumental in keeping me moving. They broke up the miles of monotony and gave me tiny goals. Four miles to here, six miles to there. While it was rare if I saw another person or any activity in town, it was that sense of progress and sense of movement I wouldn't have recognized if I was only traveling from one field of corn to the next.

I crossed the Minnesota River a half-mile past Morton, and another sign read: *Redwood Falls 7 mi.*

Those last thirty-five minutes felt like two hours. I could see the town, the water tower stood there beckoning me, but the faster I pedaled, the further the town seemed to be. Until finally, I reached the finish line. At least for day one, I was breaking through the ribbon. First place!

Welcome to Redwood Falls Est. 1864

My shoulders were shattered. Red arms, legs, and face stung from the sun. Any slight adjustment to relieve a particular pain sent agony to other parts of my body—adjust my right shoulder, my left knee would hurt; adjust my position on the saddle, my left pinky finger hurt.

My ass was tender, raw, bruised, and chafed. My quads were done, finished. Like a stubborn mule, they refused my demands.

SH 19 became East Bridge Street as it ran through Redwood Falls. As I coasted down East Bridge, I conspired with myself.

If I called Dad right now, he could be here in two or three hours and take me home.

I knew if I quit, this opportunity would be hard to come by again. I had time and money with a rebound girlfriend and a job waiting for me when I returned in sixty days.

After rolling all the way through town, I turned south onto South Washington and stopped at the post office. I dropped my pack and emptied the contents.

- Running shoes
- Three books
- Cold weather cycling jacket
- Gloves
- Dictation device and four blank tapes to record all my epic revelations I would most certainly have every moment along the empty backroads.
- Cooking stove and gas canister
- Mess kit
- Bike handlebar flashlight—a gift from the rebound girlfriend
- Towel
- Five shirts
- Jeans
- Bike lock
- Running clothes
- Teva sandals

I looked at my running shoes and clothes. They were fairly worn, so when I tossed them in the garbage bin, I didn't think twice.

The cold weather cycling jacket, gloves, jeans, and two of the shirts were packed up in a box purchased at the post office and shipped to my cousin Freddy in Boulder, Colorado. I would need warm clothes whilst overtaking the Rockies.

I poured out the white gas in my MSR fuel canister and packed it up along with my WhisperLite stove, mess kit, dictation device, tapes, and books. This package went back to Dad's.

I had one T-shirt, one pair of shorts, a pair of Teva sandals, a bike lock, a handlebar-mounted light, and plenty of newfound space, which allowed me to put my sleeping bag, tent, and towel in the pack. Best of all, I was able to strap the pack to the rack instead of having to carry it on my shoulders.

As I walked out of the post office—looking, I'm sure, weak, lost, frail, empty, and smelling disgusting—a woman approached me.

"Are you okay?" she asked, clearly concerned.

"Biking." I was a bit confused. The world around me was starting to fade. "Biking… across… California… Hotel… Food…"

Only later did I realize that my body was in hypoglycemic shock. I was on the verge of passing out from exhaustion.

"You look very hot. Do you have a place to stay?" She followed me as I moved forward with my bike toward a large patch of grass across the street. "I work at the church around the corner. It closes in five minutes, but I will leave the basement door open for you if you want to cool off and have some water. You can sleep there tonight if you'd like."

"Okay..." I said, still half-stunned. "You're very nice... thank you."

I crossed the street, found the church, and collapsed in the grass under a large oak. The world spun, faded, and then went black.

When I woke up, I saw a giant sign that read: *Church of Christ.* Lying there on a well-groomed piece of grass in Middle America, I would have preferred that the sign read: *Wang's Chinese Take-out.*

I wasn't feeling well at all—dehydrated, heat exhausted, and sunburnt. My fatigued muscles began to spasm due to an imbalance of electrolytes. The nap did help me regain some sense of where I was, although the process was slow. My quads would knot up anytime I tried to move. Finally, I was able to stand, then balance, then ride my bike, then make relatively adult decisions like locating Chinese food and a motel.

Lucky for me, the Chinese takeout was on the same block as the motel. I ordered egg rolls, hot and sour soup, and beef lo mein—extra spicy with no vegetables. I waited uncomfortably in the reception area, staring at the Maneki-neko's right arm bobbing up and down. It was hypnotic. Like the subconscious power of "The Tell-Tale Heart," the cat's tick-tocking grew louder and louder, removing my conscious mind from my body and allowing me to focus on something other than the pain that throbbed and surged through every muscle fiber.

These "beckoning cat" figurines first appeared in Japan two thousand years ago. Once upon a time, despite not having enough food to feed himself, a poor shop owner took in a starving stray cat. To show its gratitude, the cat sat in the front of the store beckoning customers, thus bringing prosperity to the charitable shop owner. Since then, the familiar cat figurine had become a symbol of good luck for small business owners. The Chinese later shanghaied the idea.

Food in hand, I slowly made my way over to the motel. Entering the office, I could smell the attendant's curry wafting up from the room behind the front desk. I was ready to tear into my takeout. The attendant was very friendly and eager to collect my thirty-eight dollars. In exchange, he handed me the key and the TV remote control for room number seven.

Inside the room, in what felt like one singular, balletic movement, I put the food on the dresser, leaned the bike against the wall, turned on the wall-mounted AC unit, and collapsed onto the bed.

Thirty minutes later, I woke up with drool running down my face and one eye cracked toward the window.

"What am I doing?" I asked no one. "Shit, man."

I kicked off my shoes, stood up, and turned on the TV. Then, I peeled off my clothes and entered the shower. Legend had it they could hear me scream as far down as room number twelve when the water found my chafed and sunburned parts. The bar of soap slipped out of my hands. The effort it would have taken to reach down and grab it hardly seemed worth it. I rinsed my jersey and shorts, the water black. I felt like I had just fought a twelve-day battle, and it was only day one.

Dripping wet and totally naked, I walked out of the bathroom, sat down on the bed, stared at the TV, glanced at the AC that was doing nothing in the way of cooling the room, then started in on the egg rolls. After the last noodle of lo mein and final drop of MSG was consumed, I discarded the empty container on the dresser next to the TV chained to the wall.

Still naked, I stood up and stared at myself in the mirror: red arms, red legs, red face, white torso.

"Really?" I asked my reflection. "You're exhausted, sunburnt, and naked in a thirty-eight-dollar motel in Redwood-f'ing-Falls, Minnesota. And you think this is a good idea?"

I questioned the whole point of the trip. Was there even a point? I was done before I had even started. I had experienced nothing. I had gone less than 5% of the way and just wanted to give up.

"You're useless!" I yelled at the shitty AC unit, or maybe to myself. "I don't even know why I'm talking to you. You don't care what I say." Then, to avoid stumbling onto some kind of realization, I clarified, "You're just a fucking air conditioner! A terrible one!"

As I laid back in bed and drifted off to sleep, my final thought was that I wanted more egg rolls.

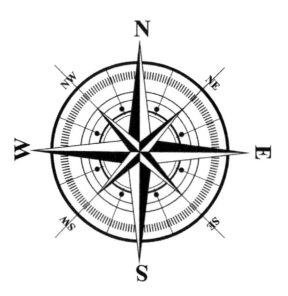

CHAPTER 2

DAY TWO

AUGUST 23, 2001

Today's Ride: Redwood Falls, Minnesota - Pipestone, Minnesota
Today's Distance: 87 Miles

"When you pray with this pipe, you pray for and with everything."

—BLACK ELK

The AC churned out no cooling comfort the entire night. The bed cover and sheets littered the floor. I lay fully spread across the queen-size bed, one pillow placed under my left knee to help alleviate the ongoing arthritic pain, the other supporting my head.

The water-stained ceiling of this worn-down, broken-air-conditioning, leaky-shower motel room offered little in the way of motivation. The room smelled of stale cigarette smoke, something I hadn't noticed the night before. I suppose for thirty-eight dollars a room, I shouldn't be surprised by the lingering smell of Pall Malls.

I was sure the sheets hadn't been changed since the previous guest's visit. Some effort made, perhaps, to brush off the pizza crumbs, tighten the edges, and tuck in the corners to give the illusion of cleanliness. Who was going to complain to the BBB? These rooms were for brief affairs, high schoolers losing their virginity, criminals on the run—nervously smoking packs of non-filtered Pall Malls and sipping from fifths of off-brand whiskey.

People made so many assumptions when checking into hotels and motels. They assumed the towels were fresh, the toilet seat had been wiped down in a sanitized manner, the glasses, if not wrapped in plastic, had been cleaned with hot, soapy water—God only knew what sort of shit lived on the remote.

After considering the petri dish I currently called home, I decided to spend a few more minutes lying in bed—too late to worry about cleanliness at that point. I scratched my already peeling sunburns and inspected my nether regions. I could feel the wounds from yesterday's battle starting to fester.

I slid out of bed and into my cycling shorts, all in one motion. Opening the door, I stood staring at East Bridge Street, showing off my pasty white torso to the morning commuters. I picked the sleep out of my eyes and flung it on the cracked *bitumen macadam*[8] outside my door in the parking spot where my car should have been.

I didn't have a car anymore. On the way to storing it, two days prior to leaving on this voyage, my 1971 cherry red Karmann Ghia and I were T-boned by some lady who ran a red light. As luck would have it, she had no license or insurance or proof of citizenship. Her male companion jumped out of the car after the impact and bolted.

Concussed and bleeding from my brow after hitting the metal dashboard, I stared at my little Ghia with sadness. It provided little

---

8　Fancy way of saying asphalt in an effort to impress you, the reader.

in the way of comfort or power, but I really dug that car. Crestfallen, I watched the Ghia get towed away and waited for a friend to pick me up.

The Volkswagen Karmann Ghia was arguably the sexiest car on the planet—this was my third one. However, it was the worst car to own if you lived in a state that produced negative-degree temps. The heat from a Karmann Ghia engine, located in the back, was blown forward through a hollow channel under the car. On any given winter day in the Upper Midwest, the "heat" would be cold again by the time it arrived upfront.

Built on top of the classic VW Bug chassis, the sleek body allowed the Ghia to reach speeds of eighty miles per hour, although I doubted I ever managed to get any of mine to go that fast. The Ghia was the brainchild of Carrozzeria Ghia, who designed the car and then approached Wilhelm Karmann to build it in 1954. VW embraced the sexy yet powerless vehicle with humor when it advertised it in the United States. One ad proudly displayed the Ghia with a racing stripe along with the tag line, "You'd lose."

I planned on buying a car when I got home from California. Something more practical, perhaps a Toyota. I wasn't really a car guy, never understood the Ford-Chevy rivalry. The first car I bought put me back $350. It had over 300,000 miles on it. "Highway miles," the seller had told his young and naive buyer. It was a tan, manual Ford Fiesta, and I did all the maintenance myself. Alternator went out, a simple trip to the junkyard and $15, and I'd have it up and running again. Then, one fateful day around 385,000 miles, the front tie rod broke. I donated it to the vo-tech, moved to Minneapolis, and didn't own a car for a couple of years, opting to walk to work as my office and world were just five blocks from my apartment.

It was around seven-thirty in the morning. Redwood Falls was bustling, and—somehow—I felt mildly rejuvenated. Surprising, considering the condition I was in just eleven and a half hours earlier. The weather was perfectly cool, the air sticky with humidity, the sun sparkling behind the lace of clouds that would soon melt away. It promised to be another warm day. I knew that if I called a friend, they could be here in an hour to pick me up and put an end to this idiocy.

I turned on the TV for background noise. A news anchor was talking about some French guy who managed to parachute into the Statue of Liberty and was currently hanging from the torch. Standing half-naked in the doorway of a shitty thirty-eight-dollar motel room in Redwood Falls, I realized my situation—having to ride another day—was far better than dangling from the torch of the Statue of Liberty.

I checked the pressure in the tyres. The front was good—93 psi. The rear was down to 88 psi. I pulled out my Topeak Road Morph hand pump and went to work pumping up the rear tyre until the gauge read 95 psi.

The Topeak Road Morph pump was fourteen inches long, one inch in diameter, and weighed half a pound. It had a built-in pressure gauge capable of reaching 160 psi, and a fold-out foot pad to help hold the pump steady for better leverage. This pump was the best tool I brought with me, so much so that to this day, I had sung its praises with the same exuberance as Ralphie Parker talking about his official Red Ryder carbine action, 200-shot, range model air rifle.

With my pack bungeed onto the rack, weight distributed as equally as possible, load considerably lighter, and water bottles filled, I walked out the door. I left the air conditioning unit running, partly out of spite and partly imagining it might simply expire and never give anyone false hopes of a cool night's sleep again.

I dropped off the key at the office, coasted over to the south side of East Bridge Street, and started pedaling. East Bridge Street turned into West Bridge Street, then back to Minnesota State Highway 19.

The stitching where the edge of chamois was sewn into my cycling shorts had already etched a ring of redness into my butt cheeks, which would eventually evolve into a scab and then a callus. Even without the pack on my back, I could hardly bring myself to sit completely in the saddle. The damage was done. All I could do was endure the pain and complain about it—aloud—while riding the shoulder of SH 19. Even if there had been someone around to hear me, they probably wouldn't have cared.

I rode standing for as long as I could, occasionally easing myself down into the saddle only to dart back up again from the pain. Finally, my legs began to fail me, and I could stand no more.

The pain of sitting in the saddle was immense. I had to constantly adjust. First, I put pressure only on the right butt cheek, then the left. Back to the right, then left, right, left... and then I would stand until my legs burned. I repeated that busted-ass dance for miles.

I knew if I suffered through the pain, one day—hopefully in the near future, if I didn't decide to bag the whole ride—the pain would be gone, and my life would be all wine and roses again.

I reached Vesta, Minnesota, a small town of 330 people named after the Roman virgin goddess of the hearth, home, and family.

With every pedal rotation, I wanted to quit. I kept thinking about how the trip was stupid, it was hot, and I was bored. My view was corn—corn, corn, corn. A long, never-ending, boring, flat road sliced through those fields of corn.

I stared at my cycling computer—a mile took forever. Small, self-imposed challenges helped break up the ride.

"Forty-five seconds, I'll be at that tree."

When I reached the tree, I would decide how close I came to my estimate. Then, I was onto the next challenge.

"That barn looks to be a half-mile away."

Over time, I was nailing it. Determining distance became my expertise.

A couple of miles past Vesta, a few MNDOT (Minnesota Department of Transportation) barriers blocked the road. A sign read, *NO THRU TRAFFIC – LOCAL TRAFFIC ONLY*. Next to it, a detour sign with an arrow pointing north.

I stopped, dismounted, pulled out my water bottle, and enjoyed a brief reprieve from the saddle. No traffic, no road crew, just me, your hero, alone with the crickets and the corn and a long stretch of freshly laid bituminous. So fresh, in fact, that the road stripes hadn't been painted yet. The road was wide, smooth as glass. Although it might have actually been the wind howling, I think I heard the road whisper, "Ride me."

"Who's to say I'm not local traffic?"

I replaced the water bottle and rode past the barrier, straight down the middle of the road—it was bliss.

My odometer started to work faster, and the miles clicked off rapidly. One might say something that resembled a smile formed on my face. Maybe this trip wasn't so bad.

In fact, the trip suddenly seemed like a great idea, possibly the smartest thing I'd ever done. Life was perfect. Madonna del Ghisallo, the Patron Saint of Cycling, was smiling down on me.

I swerved back and forth the width of the road doing my best impression of Marcus Sommers[9] chasing his brother David on the way to the Hell of the West.

It was all too perfect—a cool breeze, sun on my back. Just as I was about to pass—presumably—a golden field full of unicorns prancing under a rainbow, a terrible sound shattered all that was pure and good.

A group of dogs burst onto the scene. I looked around in a panic. Behind me, to my right, a squadron of hounds approached like a German Luftwaffe pursuing a damaged B-17 bomber.

I was exposed, helpless, naked, an innocent lamb in search of my shepherd. The dogs—maybe five, maybe ten, it was hard to tell in a quick, terrified glance over my shoulder—were fast and agile. Hellhounds, their hot breath straight from the fiery pits. Your hero was slow, weighed down, unprepared. The beasts could smell my fear, no doubt. My only hope for survival was the adrenaline now surging through my body—nature's nitrous oxide. I sprinted. I reached twenty-eight miles per hour, heart racing, lungs wheezing, drool hanging from my lower lip, snot pouring from my nostrils, legs burning from lactic acid. In just twenty seconds—though it felt much longer—it was over. The dogs suspended their chase and stood in the street barking, the littlest one out front.

Cory – 1

Dogs – 0

---

9   Kevin Costner's character in the 1985 movie *American Flyers*, who heads west to race the Hell of the West, a national road bike race with his brother David, but ends up dying from an aneurysm before completing the race.

Seven miles past my near-dog experience, an MNDOT pick-up truck pulled alongside me. Three guys were crammed in the front seat.

"Where you headed?" they hollered out a rolled-down passenger window.

"Pipestone," I yelled back.

"If you're planning to go south on 59, you might want to just go straight to 23 instead."

"Why's that?"

"59's busy with road crews and equipment."

"Thanks, I will keep that in mind."

I hadn't looked at the map yet today. I had no idea where 59 was or where it went. Minnesota State Highway 23, however, cut diagonally southwest from Marshall to Pipestone, my stop for the day. It was a straight shot, and I had no plans to deviate from this route.

It was close to eleven in the morning when I rolled up to the stoplight at the intersection with SH 23, just outside of Marshall. At 343 miles long, Minnesota State Highway 23 was the second-longest state route. It started in Duluth and ended in Pipestone.

I turned south on SH 23, skirting Marshall, a city of thirteen thousand, and shortly came across a Perkins Restaurant.

Thirty-eight miles behind me for the day, 1,818 miles to California.

Requesting a corner booth at Perkins allowed me to keep an eye on my bike while maintaining a low profile, out of consideration for the other patrons. No one wanted to sit next to or, for that matter, *look* at some dude with sweat dripping off his arms and legs, and snot hanging from his nose—the remnants of a downright epic escape from the hounds.

Dogs hadn't been something I'd even considered when I left. I didn't think I'd have to evade anything. I was biking. Nobody bothered cyclists, or so I thought. We were the purest, most advanced form of humanity on the planet. We studied, listened, smelled, embraced, learned, all at fifteen miles per hour. I'd bet most cyclists recycle. We could repair a flat tyre, get our hands greasy replacing a chain, and usually, we could even make a mean latte, too.

The waitress brought me a large glass of ice water with a menu and offered to fill my water bottles. I ordered three eggs, toast, bacon, and crispy hash browns with coffee, and left her a 50% tip.

Back on the bike for only a mile, I came across a sign that read: *Pipestone - 43 miles.*

It would only make sense that SH-23, being the second-longest road in Minnesota, would also be a busy stretch of roadway, which, as it turned out, was pretty unnerving. The upside was it offered a handsome shoulder with limited debris.

The ride was pleasant—some rolling hills, semis barreling by, some even offering a friendly honk. Though, to be honest, the first couple of friendly honks scared the shit out of me and caused me to swerve to the right instinctively to get out the way of potentially being run over.

I soon reached the town of Lynd. James W. Lynd was a pioneer and state senator who was killed during the Dakota War of 1862—or, as the roadside historical marker stated, the *Sioux Uprising*.

The town of Russell followed, then Florence, boasting a population of sixty-eight.

Just outside of Florence, I stopped to take a photo of the massive wind farm behind the hills. Nearby, grazing cows stopped to watch me, as did two guys in a white windowless van. It was the sort of van you were told to avoid as a child because there might have been a Chester[10] inside. It was also one you should be leery of as an adult, especially when you were all alone on a bicycle in the middle of nowhere.

---

10 A term for a pedophile. "Chester the child molester."

The two guys stared at me. I nervously pretended not to notice. Who were they? Just two guys getting stoned? Maybe they were meeting up for a rendezvous, forbidden by the conventions of rural Minnesota? Could they be CIA, looking for another victim to force into their MK-Ultra program?[11] Perhaps this trip was some sort of elaborate CIA mind-control experiment, pulling me west only to end up in Operation Midnight Climax[12] Part II.

After a few minutes, they drove off... or did they?

Ruthton, although small and unassuming with a population of just over three hundred, hid its dark chapter down a dirt road in an old farmhouse.

In 1983, Jim Jenkins lost everything he had to the bank. Convincing his son Steven to help him seek out revenge, Jim managed to lure Rudy Blythe, the bank president, and Deems "Toby" Thulin, his loan officer, to their now vacant farm, pretending to be interested buyers.

Like fish in a barrel, Rudy and Toby were gunned down by father and son.

A manhunt ensued, and Jim ended up cornered in a field in Texas, where he opted for a mouthful of shotgun rather than capture. Steven, just eighteen, was caught and convicted of the murders. He was released from prison in 2015.

---

11 CIA program where human subjects were given LSD in order to force confessions through mind control.
12 CIA safehouses where sex workers on the CIA payroll would seduce men and secretly give them LSD while agents monitored behavior behind one-way glass.

Aside from that bit of excitement, Ruthton didn't have much to offer by way of distraction.

A few more miles and a Shell station just off SH-23 drew me in. I grabbed a sandwich and a Gatorade and sat at the single table to eat my lunch. On the other side of the table was a guy about sixty-five, I guessed. He had a southern drawl, but one that seemed to have come and gone over the years, making it hard to distinguish if he was from the Carolinas, Mississippi, or southeast Iowa.

"Where you headed?" he asked while doing some paperwork. He didn't bother to look up.

"California."

"Wow, that's where I'm headed. I'm delivering that truck out there."

Outside sat a 2000 Peterbilt, sky blue with gold pin-striping. I stared at it, wondering where exactly I could put my bike to join him on his delivery, riding to California in comfort.

"Is that what you do, deliver trucks?"

"I do now. Me and the wife are retired, and I enjoy driving across the country. My daughter went to school in Australia. She wrote me how neat Australia was. I told her America was by far a greater country. Course, she wouldn't know. She never left the state until she went to Australia."

"Does your wife still work?"

"Oh, she likes to garden. We moved to Pennsylvania, and she has a big garden there."

"You live with her?"

"Oh yeah. She would rather garden than drive around the country with me, though. We been married for thirty-six years."

I finished my Gatorade and shook his hand on my way out.

"Have a safe ride to San Francisco," he said. "I'll tell 'em you're coming."

One mile out and the sign read: *Pipestone - 16 miles.* Behind me, a semi honked its horn—my buddy from the Shell station.

One hour later, standing on a stone base, a wood-framed sign read: *WELCOME TO PIPESTONE - PEACE PIPES, PIONEERS, AND PROGRESS.*

Considered to be sacred ground, this land served as a neutral territory where all Indian Nations could come to quarry the sacred catlinite stone without war. They used the stone to make peace pipes; the smoke from the pipe was believed to carry prayers to the Great Spirit.

The Great Spirit was the supreme being, the power of all that was universal. Known to the Sioux as *Wakan Tanka*—the great mystery.

It was close to three in the afternoon when I found myself standing at the intersection of Eighth Avenue and Seventh Street in downtown Pipestone. It wasn't Hollywood and Vine, that was for sure. But all I wanted was a hotel with working air conditioning, a shower, and some food.

The intersection offered a McDonald's, and there, like a pot of gold at the end of the rainbow, stood the GrandStay Hotel and Suites.

Considering Pipestone was a town of 4,300, the parking lot was surprisingly full. When inquiring about a room for the night, it turned out they were sold out. My heart sank. Did they not know I was in the process of what might go down in history as the greatest expedition since Lewis & Clark?

It was the start of an annual weekend of tournaments and events at Pipestone Golf & Country Club—couple's golf, Calcutta, horse racing, and a men's club tournament.

Well, *whoop-de-do*.

I had my tent, but I wasn't interested in spending any more time on my bike looking for a campsite. It was just too hot.

I walked to the corner and looked back north.

Although far from the Kunlun Mountains,[13] I found my very own Shangri-La right there on Eighth Avenue Northeast in Pipestone, Minnesota.

America's Best Value Inn had a room with a king bed, a non-leaking shower, and—most importantly—a working air conditioner. Perhaps, there was a God.

I checked in, grabbed my key card, pedaled two blocks north to a Subway, and ordered two-foot-long Spicy Italians—extra mayo. I returned to the blessed America's Best Value Inn and boarded the elevator for the second floor—bike, pack, and sandwiches all in tow.

Once inside my room, I leaned the bike against the wall, kicked off my shoes, and plopped down on the bed, then flipped on the TV.

---

13 One of the longest mountain ranges in Asia and the name of the mountain believed to be the Taoist paradise. Also, the location of Shangri-La in James Hilton's book *Lost Horizon*.

Turns out the French guy, Thierry Devaux, was rescued and arrested by New York's finest. His failed stunt had apparently been an effort to protest the use of land mines.

I took a deep breath—another day of riding was behind me. Two feet of meat, mayo, and bread were consumed in under fifteen minutes. The room was finally cool, my skin was scorched, and my belly was full. I lay back and stared at the smoke detector, its blinking light drawing me into a hypnotic sleep.

SOUTH DAKOTA

"Friend"

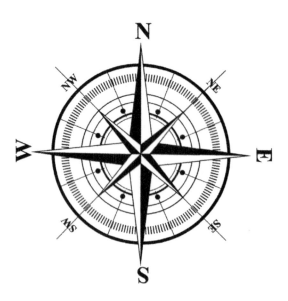

CHAPTER 3

DAY THREE

AUGUST 24, 2001

Today's Ride: Pipestone, Minnesota - Sioux Falls, South Dakota
Today's Distance: 63 Miles

> "The most effective way to do it is to do it."
>
> —AMELIA EARHART

On August 24, 1932, Amelia Earhart woke up, enjoyed a few Lucky Strikes, studied some aeronautical charts, put on her white leather flying helmet, and took off from Los Angeles, California, for a 2,447 mile, solo, non-stop flight to Newark, New Jersey in her bright red Lockheed Vega 5B, affectionately named Little Red Bus. And she did it in a record time of nineteen hours.

On August 24, 2001—sixty-nine years later—your hero awoke at America's Best Value Inn in Pipestone, Minnesota, with absolutely no ambition to continue his bike ride. Reluctantly, he pulled on his dirty red cycling jersey and stinky black Lycra shorts, slipped on his socks, and slid on his shoes. He strapped his pack to the rack on his bike, then pushed his 1999 Specialized Allez—which had not yet been named with any sort of affection—two hundred yards to the McDonald's. He ordered a couple of Sausage McMuffins and an orange juice. After which, he pulled out his *Rand McNally, Easy To Read: North Dakota, South Dakota* foldable highway map. He carefully studied how he was going to make it sixty-three miles south-by-southwest to Sioux Falls, South Dakota, by the end of the day. He had no intention of breaking any record times, if any existed.

Riding west on Minnesota State Highway 30, the miles ticked off slower and slower.

Stopping in the middle of a field, I stared at the road ahead of me. Reaching California seemed impossible. However, it dawned on me that this road would connect to another road, and then another in a seamless network of asphalt that would guide me to California.

Behind me was Pipestone. If I wanted to, I could turn around and be back there in less than an hour—find a restaurant, enjoy a nice meal, call someone to pick me up, and be home by dinner.

Who would I call? What would I tell everyone who I boasted to about this event? Would I go back to work on Monday? Why would I do that? Why would I throw away an approved two-month leave of absence? What about my friends? Oh sure, friends would support me, but *real* friends? Real friends would give me shit for years about how I didn't even make it out of Minnesota.

Perhaps I could devise a story.

☑ Road bandits stopped me at gunpoint at the border of South Dakota and stole my bike and all my gear, leaving me naked along the side of the road. I survived off raw corn and grubs for two hours until I was rescued by a fourteen-year-old operating a $240,000 combine.

- ☑ An unnamed family member became sick and I needed to return directly home. My very presence was the lifeblood they needed to heal.

- ☑ Abducted by aliens. Every future March 20[14] would be spent at the Extraterrestrial Abduction Day festival, competing in the *Close Encounters of the Third Kind* Devil's Tower shaving cream sculpture contest, and discussing whether or not a special pair of sunglasses could detect aliens.

I looked at my shoes then up to the sky, searching for Foo Fighters. Nothing, not even a contrail.

Instead of all that, I pushed on and made it to the South Dakota border. Supported by two galvanized U-channel posts stood a big, boring, white-trimmed green sign with white letters reading: *Welcome to South Dakota*. Backroad state line border crossings apparently didn't get the same exciting signage fanfare as they did at interstate crossings.

No matter, the aesthetic of the sign was far less important to me than the words. This sign gave me the boost I needed to continue forward. I stopped my bike and read the words aloud.

"South Dakota. Great Faces. Great Places."

Before I left Minneapolis, I was talking with one of my co-workers who was a cyclist. I remember telling him, "Man, this trip is going to be awesome. I get to ride my bike all day for thirty days!"

14 National Alien Abduction Day.

How naive I was and how much wiser now. I was just starting my third day and already conjuring up a plan to end all this cycling *awesomeness*.

Armed with my Olympus Stylus Zoom 140 35mm camera, marketed as "the camera that embodies all the latest technology," I took a picture of my bike leaning against the sign. Then, I pedaled west on South Dakota Highway 34 with great enthusiasm.

Highway 34 stretched the length of the state, 419 miles. If I decided to continue straight west, I could cycle along SH-34 into Wyoming and be there in just over four days. My goal wasn't Wyoming. For the short term, my goal was Interstate 29, just sixteen miles west. Then I'd finish the day—and possibly my ride—in Sioux Falls, South Dakota, thirty-six miles south of there.

The newfound enthusiasm I experienced at the border started to dwindle as I crossed the Big Sioux River and completely diminished as I reached the town of Egan. I spent a brief moment admiring the grain silos and then continued on.

A couple of miles west, I reached a sign erected in 1956 by the M.W.C. Club and the state highway commission:

"The Lone Tree"

"Here on the Highway, in front of this marker, stood the 'LONE TREE' for more than two generations. It was planted a mere cottonwood seedling in the hole left by pulling out the original survey stake (surveyed in September 1869 by Levi P. Drake and crew) at the corner of the NE quarter of Section 20 Township 106 N Range 49 E which was homesteaded by George Cameron in 1880. Mrs. Cameron planted the seedling in 1881, little thinking that this tiny seedling would grow into a stately tree, which would be a beacon signal in a blizzard to save the life of a teacher, Emma Clancy, and her little flock of twelve children; nor did she think its existence later would provoke a terrific controversy as to its preservation as a landmark when a paved highway came under the shelter of its wide-spreading branches. Emaciated by this concrete-created drought about its roots, causing the tree to die, this marker is dedicated to preserve the memory of a famous landmark."

The Lone Tree was a victim of South Dakota's tree removal program.

One could prepare for many things. One could prepare for climbing hills by doing hill repeats or for wind by riding in it. One could even build up a resistance to rain and snow. I, of course, spent no time training or preparing for any of these things. However, what I was completely unprepared for was the overwhelming sense of loneliness.

Thomas Wolfe wrote: "Loneliness, far from being a rare and curious phenomenon, peculiar to myself and a few solitary men, is a central and inevitable fact of human existence."

There was the stranded-on-a-deserted-island, happy-you-survived-whatever-wreckage-caused-you-to-be-there lonely.

Then, there was the self-imposed loneliness, knowing you were just one call away from rescue.

I was on a self-imposed island. It wasn't deserted, but it felt that way sometimes. In 1991, after my sophomore year at college, I got a job on Wake Island, where I was part of an island restoration project. We demoed a few old buildings that were abandoned after the 1970s. A small group of civilians had lived there and managed air traffic until the FFA took over in 1972. My first job was driving a dump truck. Eventually, my responsibilities evolved, and I ended up running the only D7 bulldozer and front-end loader on the island. Technically, Wake Island was an atoll—one that sat in the Pacific Ocean, 2,298 miles west of Hawaii and 2,000 miles southeast of Tokyo. The atoll was one of the remotest places on the planet and was always one typhoon away from disappearing.

We worked ten-hour days, six days a week. I spent my off time alone, staring at the massive Pacific Ocean, feeling completely isolated. We had no internet and a phone call was three dollars a minute. I brought two cassettes with me—The Police's *Synchronicity* and Enigma's *MCMXC a.D.* Not exactly the two best cassettes to be stuck with for four months if you needed a pick me up. To add salt to that wound, the guy who ran the one TV channel—if you wanted to call it that—only ran—and I swear this to be true—the movie *Internal Affairs* with Richard Gere, Andy Garcia, and Nancy Travis. Not sure why that was, but...it was. To avoid that, I spent my evenings at the only bar on the atoll—Drifters Reef.

It was a pretty remarkable experience, aside from working with a handful of rough fellas from the Louisiana State Penitentiary who wouldn't think twice about putting a knife in you if you looked at them sideways. One day, I ran over a bunch of nails with the work truck and was yelled at, rightly so, by the boss man. Afterward, one of those ex-convicts said to me, "If he yelled at me like that, I would have killed him." I believed he was very serious.

I learned to SCUBA, which for those of you who might not know, is an acronym for Self-Contained Underwater Breathing

Apparatus. Sundays, during low tide, were spent catching spiny lobsters by hand in the coral reefs. A few of us would get together afterward for a nice lobster dinner. Sneaky Pete—one of our co-workers—would provide the Black Velvet Whisky. Pete was the only guy I ever met who got so drunk he fell UP the stairs. He drank 750 ml of Black Velvet a day, smoked non-filtered Lucky Strikes, and had, as he liked to say, "an altitude problem."

Spiny lobster catch of the day

Although I never returned to college after Wake Island, the experience drilled into me that I had to make some better life choices. It also showed me that although I was working and living on one of the most isolated atolls in the world, the world had a lot to show me. I knew then I needed to work—if only so I could roam.

Back on the bike, my motivation to get to California was gone. I left that on the side of the road, five miles back, next to a dead raccoon.

I was physically tired; my butt was in constant pain…but I had to keep grinding out miles. It wasn't the physical suffering that was holding me back; it was the mental. I was all wrapped up in my head and in there was a constant battle—devil on one shoulder, angel on the other.

Twenty-four days? Thirty-two days? Eighty days? I really didn't know how long it would take me to get to California. I came up with the estimated number of days based on a simple math problem: two thousand miles divided by seventy-five miles a day, on average, would equal twenty-seven days.

The fields of produce represented nothing but loneliness. It was me alone with the sun, crickets, and corn.

The road led me deeper into loneliness. I pedaled away from and toward nowhere. The road stayed with me, always with me. I chased a vanishing point that I could never catch. Looking back, the road would show me where I had been. Forward or backward, the view was all the same.

By the time I reached Interstate 29, I pretty much had all the logistics figured out: I'd leave my bike in Sioux Falls and take a Greyhound to Denver, Colorado. I didn't want to do this anymore. Alone on this bicycle out here under the forever sky, unwanted, unknown, unaccepted, unappreciated.

What was the point? What was I trying to prove, if anything? It was just a poorly planned idea that I threw into action because it was a beautiful day in August. Why go on? To wrestle with me every moment of the day, convince myself to move forward while hammering out the logistics of how to conclude this meaningless exploit?

I had a plan to travel the world when I was thirty. Give it all up, sell everything, and go. But I struggled with the idea. My career was going well. I had everything I didn't need but thought I did—two houses, two cars, two motorcycles, an unnecessary wardrobe.

One day, I had headed out for a run, and a guy by the name of Don Kingston, aged seventy-four, was also preparing for a run. We met originally as members of a marathon training group. He was the only septuagenarian I knew with earrings. I asked him if he wanted to run together. I had a question that required an older, wiser person's perspective.

"Don, I'm thirty-one and want to travel the world, but I'm concerned I might be risking my career."

He told me the following story as we started out on our first mile:

"Cory, my wife and I married in 1949, and our plan was to travel around Europe for six months. As a wedding gift, my aunt gave us two thousand dollars, which was a tremendous amount of money at the time. We decided to take the money and put a down payment on a house, telling ourselves we would go to Europe on our first anniversary. Our first anniversary arrived, and we opted to buy furniture for the house, telling ourselves we would go to Europe the next year."

He paused and looked at me.

"Cory, I'm seventy-four years old, and I've never been to Europe."

Here I was, traveling. But it felt like I was doing nothing but killing time. Filling my days biking. A grown man on a bicycle. It wasn't what grown men did. Grown men worked, provided for their families, took up hobbies, such as woodworking or fixing up a car from the year they were born. They maxed out their 401(k)s, went to happy hours with colleagues, and watched the nightly news with a glass of Scotch to conclude their day.

Grown men spent their weekends at Home Depot searching for hoses and light bulbs. They pretended to like their neighbor, so they could borrow their weed whacker.

Day three and just twenty miles into my ride, I was already tapping out. I'd spend today getting myself to Sioux Falls. Once there, I'd lock the bike up in front of a public building, the post office or library. Someplace easy to find and fully exposed to prevent it from being stolen or vandalized.

Then, I would call my brother and offer him a couple hundred dollars to come and get my bike while I traveled to Denver in relative comfort by way of a Greyhound.

From Denver, I'd call my cousin, have him pick me up, and spend a few days in Boulder. After that, I'd formulate a plan to get me to California. Maybe I'd buy a motorcycle or a car. I needed a new car anyway. Maybe I'd take a train through the mountains. I had no game plan, but now I had options. It was the right thing to do. Grown men didn't ride bicycles.

I could see for dozens of miles in all directions. The land was flat and boring. The only interruption that offered any excitement was the sign in front of me that read: *Colman 3 miles.*

Colman was west of I-29. I could make it out in the distance and decided it would be a good place to take a break. Hash out the details of my new plan on a napkin at the local eatery. I could find the library, one that was open and had a public computer. Then, I could get online, find the address of the Greyhound bus terminal in Sioux Falls, and figure out when the next bus left for Denver.

Pedaling toward Colman, I continued to convince myself of why this whole idea of biking to California was just stupid. No one cared if I made it. There was no medal for crossing the finish line. There was no finish line. Colman could be the end if I so chose.

Welcome to the City of COLMAN - Established 1880

Colman was a town of eleven streets, 578 people, and Looney Days, which offered "Food & Fun for Everyone," according to the brochure. Other than the obvious signs of modern human development—cars, houses, power lines—one might have taken Colman for abandoned.

Turning north on Main Street, I pulled up to the Colman Community Center, which also served as the senior citizens' center and library.

It was a modest, unassuming, brown, wood-framed building. I leaned my bike against the outside wall, feeling confident that it would still be there when I returned. I had yet to see another soul. I opened the glass door at the front of the building and stepped into a hallway. Immediately to my left was a door that read: *Senior Citizens.* I peered in. A group of six women was making quilts, talking, and laughing.

"Excuse me," I said, aware of how jarring my presence must have been. "Where is the library?"

"Last door on the left," one of the ladies responded.

The library was a small room, the size of a two car garage. Two women sat at a table in the center of the room.

"Can I help you?" the librarian asked.

"Yes, do y'all have email?"

"Yes, we do, just sign in here."

Against the wall was a brand-new computer. It looked untouched. I sat down and logged on.

"Looks like you're biking somewhere?" the librarian asked.

"Yep, heading to California."

"Oh my, where did you come from?"

"Minneapolis."

"All the way from Minneapolis? Well, that is something. How long did it take you?"

"I'm on my third day, trying to get to Sioux Falls today."

"Well, Sioux Falls is pretty far away. Would you like some coffee?"

"No, thank you."

Logging onto the Greyhound web page, I found a bus that left Sioux Falls daily at 9:30 p.m. for seventy-seven dollars, one way. It would be a nineteen-hour twenty-minute trip that would take me through the towns of Vermillion, South Dakota; Omaha, Nebraska; Lincoln, Nebraska; Aurora, Nebraska; and Sterling, Colorado, before arriving in Denver at 6:50 a.m. the next day.

The bus was looking more and more promising as an alternative plan. I mean, I'd never been to Aurora, Nebraska. Bet you didn't know Aurora, Nebraska, was the hometown of the man who invented the strobe light, Harold Edgerton. Fascinating stuff. Indeed, this trip modification was growing legs.

I shut down the computer, thanked the librarian, walked out to my bike, and headed back east on SD-34, then turned south on 472nd Avenue. It was a long stretch, which couldn't have been a better representation of my increasing depression and loneliness.

Five miles later, I turned back east on 240th Street. I was back-tracking two miles east, but this route appeared to be the quickest and easiest way to Sioux Falls. A couple of miles down, I turned south again on 474th Avenue and rode the six miles into Dell Rapids, South Dakota, "the little city with the big attractions."

The only attraction that managed to get my attention was the T & C service station, which sat next to a Dairy Queen.

With just twenty-three miles left before reaching Sioux Falls, I opted for another bottle of Gatorade and a horrible slice of dried-out pizza. I could only imagine the pizza had been sitting on a paper board under a rotating heat lamp for the past two hours.

I took my place outside on the concrete curb—in one hand, a warm slice of pizza; in the other, a fruit punch Gatorade. I was hungry, not a sommelier. The slice of pizza left me wondering what gut-wrenching damage lay in store for me five miles down the road.

I was excited about the whole idea of the Greyhound. No more headwind, no more corn, no more cows, dogs, or semi-trailers, no more rumble strips or roadkill or debris. No more boredom. No more loneliness.

Then, I thought about the librarian back in Colman, how she was impressed that I was biking to California. The Greyhound also meant there would be no more pedaling, fresh air, amazing sunsets, or the sense of accomplishment after a long hard day of riding. No more Gatorade and shitty food. No more telling people, "I'm cycling to California."

I gulped down my drink and started questioning my escape plan. Maybe I didn't want to quit. I took a two-month leave of absence. I had time.

Before leaving on my bike ride, I sold my first house and rented out my second. I went from having $87.34 in my checking account and no savings to having six figures in my savings account with rental income rolling in. I felt like a king.

Did I really want to quit? Maybe not just yet. I had already biked hundreds of miles—222 to be exact. That in and of itself was an accomplishment. By the end of the day, I would have cycled a total of 248 miles.

I had twenty-six miles and a night in Sioux Falls to figure it out. Currently, jumping on the Greyhound was leading by a solid 80%, but my ego was chipping away at that number.

Sioux Falls was less than two hours away. I planned on arriving around 3:00 p.m. This would give me ample time to find the Greyhound station, buy a ticket, find a place to lock up my bike so my brother could pick it up, find a hotel, and have dinner.

At Dell Rapids, 274th Ave turned into South Dakota Highway 115, designated a POW/MIA Memorial Highway. I took it straight into Sioux Falls.

When I rolled under Interstate 90 and past the Love's Travel Stop, it was about 2:45 p.m. Traffic seemed light as I continued south on SD-115, now North Cliff Avenue.

I was pedaling past the Graham Tire Company, Parks Marina, St. Michael's Cemetery, Barney's Used Cars & Parts, and crossing over the Big Sioux River when it happened.

I made a last-minute attempt to avoid it, but I hit the metal street grate full-on, exploding my rear tyre. Well, the tube anyway.

That was what bike tubes did when filled with over ninety pounds of pressure…they exploded. At first, I was startled. I didn't know what to make of it. The rear of the bike wobbled back and forth as I slowed down, finally coming to a complete stop before reaching East Rice Street.

Pulling my bike off the road, I laid it down in the grass. I stretched and stared at the massive John Morrell & Co. meat processing facility.

George Morrell, a very poor and down-on-his-luck thirty-nine-year-old, lived in Bradford, England, 174 years ago. He worked as a wool comber until he inherited sixty pounds.

He paid off all his debt, kissed his comber career goodbye, and walked down to the canal boats. With the remaining money, he bought some oranges and sold them down the street at a profit. Repeating this exchange, he soon became a successful fruit merchant. Three years later, George took a leap and started curing hams and bacon. Morrell's Yorkshire Hams and Bacon not only became a successful company, but it was also considered the gold standard in Great Britain.

I stood in the shadow of George's legacy, which had landed in Sioux Falls because the railroad added easy distribution access in the new land. I looked at my bike, trying to remember what to do when one got a flat. Fortunately, I was armed with four tubes and a bike pump.

Unstrapping my pack, I tossed it aside. Then I flipped my bike upside down, pulled the rear quick-release lever, unscrewed the skewer, pulled off the wheel, and laid it down on the ground. Digging through my pack, I pulled out a tube, unraveled it, and opened the Presta valve to blow into it and get a bit of air inside. I then picked up my wheel and realized I had no tyre irons.

Not having tyre irons wasn't the end of the world, but it sure helped with the process when trying to replace a tube on a road bike. The tyres were on the rim pretty tight.

The tyre iron was a plastic tool with a flat curved end on one side and a hook that you could fasten to your spoke on the other.

They were usually four to six inches long. Ideally, you had two or three of them in case one broke. I had zero.

As kids, when we got a flat, we'd just go over to Dad's well-organized tool drawer, take one of his Craftsman flathead screwdrivers, and pry the tyre off the rim of our Schwinn Stingrays. The rim on my Stingray was steel. The rims on my Allez were Mavic CXP 23 made of 6106 aluminum alloy. I wasn't sure exactly what 6106 aluminum alloy was, but my guess was a screwdriver would no doubt destroy it. It didn't matter. I didn't have a screwdriver either.

With all my might, I managed to pry the tyre off with my fingers and pull out the tube. It was un-patchable, which didn't matter, as I didn't have a patch kit. I rolled up the blown tube and shoved it in my pack. Taking the new tube, I wrapped it around the rim and gave it a few pumps, to stiffen it up and give me something to work with. I tucked the tyre back onto the rim, a struggle which was equally as difficult without an iron as removing the tyre.

I started pumping away with my Topeak hand pump. As the gauge approached 70 psi, the tube exploded. I had pinched the tube between the tyre and the rim. A total amateur move—but I was an amateur. I was three days into a trip and had very little experience with flat tyres. I only planned on the possibility of four flats and anticipated no mechanical issues. Why would there be mechanical issues? The bike was in tip-top shape. I knew this because I had squeezed the brake levers before departing, the gears shifted when instructed to, the wheels spun... what else was there? It wasn't rocket science; it was a bicycle.

I threw my pump on the ground and started swearing. I didn't care so much about the loss of another tube. It was the thought of having to pry the tyre off the rim again that bothered me.

Inserting the second tube, I inspected the edges of the rim and tube to make sure nothing was pinching and proceeded to pump up to 95 psi. Success.

Checking the tyre to make sure it was seated properly, I slid it back into the stays, tightened up the quick release, flipped the bike back over, strapped my pack back on the rack, and proceeded west on East Rice Street, which turned into North Weber. I turned west on Falls Park Drive and crossed the Big Sioux River. Below the bridge and running alongside the river was the Sioux Falls Bike Trail. I followed it south toward the falls.

It was Friday—the stores were open late and bars were getting ready for the evening. I found a payphone and called my cousin Freddy in Boulder. Leaving a message on his voicemail, I let him know to prepare for my arrival.

Finding the Greyhound bus terminal, I purchased a ticket. The bus left at 9:30 p.m. In less than five hours, I would be on a Greyhound headed to Colorado. I was no longer excited about the prospect of the bus, but I had a non-refundable bus ticket—the die was cast.

Cycling back to downtown, I stopped at Crawford's Bar and Grill where I found myself horribly underdressed. Finding a stool at the bar, I ordered a celebratory shot of Maker's Mark to toast the completion of three days of cycling. Looking at myself in the mirror, I raised a glass. "Kudos to you, sir."

People began filling in the space, all arriving to celebrate the end of another work week. In the mirror, they reflected the life I was living just days prior. I was suddenly sure I didn't want to return to that, not yet. I had time to be that reflection in a mirror when I got back to Minneapolis.

I ordered another shot of whiskey. I rather enjoyed the anonymity of sitting at the bar, not participating, making up stories of who these strangers in the mirror were.

For I had bravely ridden my bike from Minneapolis, with California in my crosshairs, I told myself I was not part of that tribe. I broke away from the chains of normality while simultaneously breaking away from the chains of taking the Greyhound.

I ordered the steak, medium rare, and another whiskey. I decided I wanted to finish this adventure, but on my terms. And if that meant steak and whiskey dinners, so be it.

After I finished my meal, I gulped down a couple of pints of water and paid my tab.

It was a cool evening. I rode my bike, weaving on East Eleventh Street with one eye open, the whiskey doing its job. I dropped down on the Sioux Falls Bike Trail. It was dusk when I crossed over the second set of railroad tracks, where I decided to set up my tent. I ducked into the woods just before the basketball court in Beadle Park, pitched camp, and drifted to sleep.

NEBRASKA

"Flat Water"

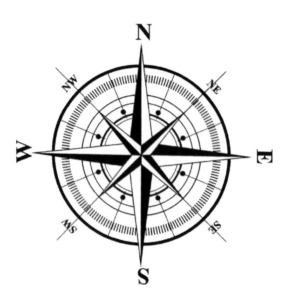

CHAPTER 4

DAY FOUR

AUGUST 25, 2001

Today's Ride: Sioux Falls, South Dakota - Grand Island, Nebraska
Today's Distance: 114 miles (plus 135 miles by car): 249 total

> "People don't take trips, trips take people."
>
> —JOHN STEINBECK

The sound of a runner passing my tent woke me up. That, and an incredible need to pee. I crawled out of my tent and found the nearest tree.

My mouth tasted like whiskey. I hadn't brushed my teeth before passing out in my sleeping bag. How I made it *into* my sleeping bag was a bit of a mystery. Somehow, I managed to set up the tent, unpack my backpack, crawl into my sleeping bag, and sleep comfortably.

My stomach gurgled. There was now a sense of urgency, as I was without toilet paper and had only one pair of socks, which could not be sacrificed.

I had three days behind me, a seventy-seven-dollar non-refundable Greyhound bus ticket, and every intention to keep biking after watching America's middle class at happy hour. The Greyhound was no longer an option. I'd have to visit Harold Edgerton's hometown another time.

I took my time packing up my tent and sleeping bag to give the sun time to catch up with me.

It was cool, overcast, and still dark, maybe 5:00 a.m. I hadn't brought a watch. I didn't need it—I was one with nature. Three days on the open road, I was a survivalist.

Thoreau identified the four necessities of life in *Walden*: food, shelter, clothing, and fuel. That was in 1854.

In 2001, I amended Thoreau's four necessities to reflect my current situation: bicycle, tent, clothing, and a debit card.

I had it all figured out. I knew that moss grew on the north side of the tree, the sun set in the west, the North Star was the tail of Ursa Minor (aka Little Bear or Little Dipper), and Orion's Belt pointed east and west. If the sun was behind me as I headed west, it was morning. If directly above me, noon. If in front of me, evening approached.

Heck, I even knew how to start a fire using flint and steel (neither of which I had in my pack, but that was beside the point). At home, I had my Grandpa Mortensen's old flint and steel kit from when he was a Boy Scout back in the 1920s. I actually did manage to make a fire using it, which was a task that generally required more patience than I was capable of having at any single time. Grandpa was big into scouting. I think he was more excited when I became an Eagle Scout than I was.

I had borrowed my buddy's tent, which, when packed up, weighed all of a single pound compressed to a mere fifteen-by-four inches. My sleeping bag was an old North Face, down-filled Blue Kazoo. I got it when I was fifteen as a reward for being selected as one of ten Boy Scouts to hike the Grand Canyon rim to rim to rim. The Blue Kazoo was a little light on the down and needed to be refilled, but I didn't anticipate any cold weather this time of year. I brought it because I could compress it down to eight-by-fourteen inches.

Before this trip, everything I thought I needed to survive fit in a four-bedroom house with four garages. Now, everything I actually needed to live fit in a forty-liter backpack.

We create our own encumbrances.

There were still fifty-seven days before I needed to be back at work. Cycling a modest fifty miles a day, I would reach California with plenty of time to spare.

I hopped on my nameless bike and followed the path north to East Tenth Street, which eventually turned into East Twelfth Street, and, ultimately, South Dakota State Highway 42. Heading west, I passed the *USS South Dakota memorial*, which was in the final stages of construction.

During its first year of duty in WWII, the *USS South Dakota* was badly damaged during battle. In an effort to make the Japanese think they had sunk her, the *USS South Dakota* was referred to as "Battleship X."

Battleship X participated in the Battle of Guadalcanal in the Solomon Sea, which, along with the Battle of Midway, was an epic turning point on the Pacific front. The Battle of Guadalcanal ended with Allies losing 7,100 men, twenty-nine ships, and 615 aircraft. Japanese lost 31,000 men, thirty-eight ships, 880 aircraft and 1,000 men captured. Guadalcanal was currently one of the greatest ship-wreck dive locations in the world.

The USS South Dakota had another notable bit of WWII trivia. Calvin Graham, who served on the ship from 1942-43, was the youngest serviceman to participate in WWII, at just twelve years old. He received a Purple Heart and Bronze Star before his age was revealed.

I couldn't imagine what life was like living on a vulnerable bat-tleship floating around the Pacific Ocean, hundreds, maybe thou-sands of miles from land, your only security blanket an even more vulnerable lifeboat. There you'd be, a slow-moving target, waiting for the enemy to sink you, if you couldn't sink them first. Planes attacked you from above; submarines snuck up on you from below.

If the enemy successfully sunk you, with the average depth of the Pacific Ocean being 12,000 feet (2.27 miles), a ship sinking at thirty miles per hour would take you to Davy Jones's Locker in five minutes. At my cycling pace, it would take me ten minutes—I rode slower than a sinking ship. That was humbling.

I was that floating ship, a small speck drifting across a sea of corn. I realized I had spent the last three days in a mental battle—Sioux Falls was my Guadalcanal, my turning point in this self-created war.

SD-42 passed a bar called Chasers. Its kiosk read: *Casual Dining, Right Price, Right Here.* I wondered what they considered the right price to be and for what. Could I get a martini for four dollars? They'd probably serve it to me in a rocks glass with a straw.

Back in the fields, it was dreary and ominous. The sky was dark grey and had the makings of a summer storm. I could smell the rain, although the rain would never come. There was something else on the way.

In Basque mythology, Egoi was the god of wind. In Finnish mythology, her name was Tuuletar. Greek, Aeolus, god and ruler of the winds. Njord, the Norse god of wind. Aztecs called him Ehecatl. Feng Po Po was the Chinese wind goddess. In Japan, her name was Shinatobe, and it was Vayu who brought the winds to the Hindu.

Just west of Sioux Falls, Egoi, Tuuletar, Aeolus, Njord, Ehecatl, Feng Po Po, Shinatobe, and Vayu all decided to get together, right here on South Dakota 42, and let me know their great power.

I didn't know how to gauge the speed of the wind, but I did know the amount of work required to ride into a headwind. Riding a bike on a flat road, with no headwind at eighteen miles per hour requires about 180 watts. With a headwind of five miles per hour, that jumps up to 230 watts—ten miles per hour equaled 286 watts; fifteen miles per hour equaled 357 watts; twenty miles per hour equaled 428 watts. Of course, other factors were, but not limited to, the weight and position of the rider.

I was kicking out eight miles per hour with an eighteen-mile-per-hour headwind, generating about 210 watts.

I found myself doing a lot of math to pass the time. Fifty miles a day at fifty-seven days was 2,850 miles. At fifteen miles per hour, that was 190 hours. If I biked 8 hours a day, that would be just under twenty-four days.

It was thirty-one miles from the *USS Dakota* to County Road 81. At eight miles per hour, fighting a headwind, that would be four hours of struggle—and let me tell you my friends, the struggle was real.

Everything was math and electricity. I was generating watts, burning calories, and traveling miles at various speeds, fighting friction and the kinetic energy of the wind, which was created by atmospheric numbers changing on a planet spinning at one thousand miles per hour.

The song of the crickets had disappeared; cornfields swayed in a fierce, rhythmic wave. Your hero, an ant on a bicycle in an ocean of cornfields, was unhappily bucking a fucking headwind.

Bucking: Opposing or resisting something that seems oppressive or inevitable.

Four hours of fighting all that science and mythology and I finally reached US-81, imagining it couldn't get any worse.

US-81, originally called the Meridian Highway, as it sat near the Sixth Principal Meridian, was unofficially part of the Pan-American Highway. The Pan-American Highway was the world's longest system of roads, stretching from Prudhoe Bay, Alaska, to Ushuaia, Argentina.

Jake Silverstein described the Pan-American Highway as: "A system so vast, so incomplete, and so incomprehensible, it is not so much a road as it is an idea of Pan-Americanism itself."

For me, US-81 looked vast, but far less a part of some massive system of Pan-Americanism. All I could see were four vanishing points framed by cornfields heading east, west, north, and south.

The following serves absolutely no point to my story:

While standing at the intersection, there were a half dozen parked cars in a dirt lot. A car coming from the east stopped and dropped off a passenger. The passenger got into one of the parked cars and both cars drove off, one going east, the other west. Another car arrived from the south, with two people. The driver got out and into another car that was already parked there and drove west, leaving the passenger to sit alone. A few moments later another car showed up with two people, from the east, the passenger got out, got into the car with the passenger who was sitting alone, and then both cars drove off south.

I started south. The wind was even was worse.

Eleven miles on, at the intersection of US-81 and US-46, a dilapidated building with two crumbling gas pumps, which appeared to be the former Creek Grill Bar Casino, stood all alone at a lonely corner on this barren stretch of road.

Its impending future? Some dude in a rusty, yellow D8 Caterpillar bulldozer scraped its empty soul from the earth to build a Kum & Go, complete with a Subway.

The wind had let up considerably. Yankton was just fourteen miles south.

I crossed over *Etazipokase Wakpa*, as the Dakota called it—"un-navigable river." Later, French explorers would change the name to *Rivière aux Jacques*, which translated to its current name, James River. It was the eighteenth longest river in the United States.

Yankton was within sight, as was the Nebraska border, when my front tyre went flat. A flat tyre was welcome. It allowed me to stop, stretch, take it all in—all that vastness.

Urban sprawl didn't exist here. People who talk of urban sprawl had never left their world of concrete and steel.

Not on a bicycle anyway, pedaling for hours only to get further into nowhere, where the lights of some city never interrupted the night sky.

The Pawnee understood the sky, this was their land. They believed the stars were gods that interacted with humans. The warrior star, Mars, mated with the female star, Venus, to create the first humans.

I made a note that I might need to buy a few more tubes, tyre irons, and maybe a patch kit when I came across a bike shop.

Standing there, holding my front wheel, surrounded by the haunting sounds of the prairie, a car stopped behind me. Perhaps a gift from Abeona,[15] I walked over to the passenger side.

"Hey man, need a ride?" He was about twenty and looked relatively harmless.

"I don't know. How far you going?" I was disoriented by our sudden conversation.

15 Roman goddess of journeys.

"Lincoln."

"Lincoln?!"

"Just get in, okay?" The driver scanned the horizon, which gave the impression he was being chased or followed, maybe escaping General Zaroff's[16] wicked game.

I looked around to see what he was looking at, or for. The road was empty, the sky was free of aircraft—no UFOs. I leaned my head back in the passenger window.

"I don't know if the bike will fit in the backseat."

"Look, that's just too bad. I have got to get going," he said, somewhat frantically.

"Okay, okay. Hold on, man."

I managed to fit the bike into the back of the car. It was a 1970-something four-door Pontiac LeMans, sans a muffler. The car reminded me of my dad's 1968 Pontiac Bonneville.

No headrests or seat belt strapped to the ceiling, the doors weighed seventy pounds and creaked when they opened and closed.

I jumped in the front seat, and before I could get the door closed, my young, paranoid chauffeur was driving us down the road, leaving a puff of black smoke in our wake.

"Sorry man, I get freaked out way out here in the country. Don't like big cities either. I'm not paranoid or anything, just get freaked out. Know what I mean?"

"No, not really. If you're so freaked out, why did you pick me up?"

---

16 In the book *The Most Dangerous Game*, Zaroff, a wealthy Russian aristocrat prefers to hunt other men, as they are "the most dangerous game."

He looked at me like I just blew his mind, then pulled out a joint and turned up the tunes.

"Why are you so scared of the country?"

He ignored me and slid in a CD.

"How do you deal with living in the city if you're so freaked out?"

"Ever heard of The String Cheese Incident?"

"No."

"This band is incredible, man. I'm studying music at the University of Nebraska at Lincoln. Listen to that, do you hear it?"

"Yeah, sure, I hear *that*." I was playing in his sandbox, no need for me to be rude. I leaned back in the seat and stuck my hand out the window, allowing the wind to move it up and down. I wondered about this kid. What did his future have in store? How did he muster the balls to pull over on a deserted stretch of road to pick up a random cyclist, as paranoid as he was?

He sparked up the joint, then switched the CD, putting in Steve Miller Band's *Greatest Hits*. Someone had upgraded the radio in the car with a CD player and digital display, but the speakers were still original Delcos.

"Listen to this," my driver said. "He had to be on acid when he wrote this song. Listen. See what I mean, man?"

The song was "Fly Like an Eagle."

"So, how long have you been biking?"

"This is my fourth day."

"There's no way I would be alone in the country, man, you're

crazy. These people out here…I'm not paranoid. It's just these people, you know?"

He took another hit.

"How many miles you bike a day?"

"About one hundred."

"No way! Lance Armstrong can't even bike that far dude."

Lance had just won his third Tour de France, but I wasn't sold
on him. My guy was Greg LeMond, the first and only US American
to win the Tour de France as Lance Armstrong was later stripped
of all his "victories" as was US American Floyd Landis of his 2006
victory.

I was sixteen when LeMond won his first Tour de France in
1986, and his international success influenced me to take up cycling.
Not competitively, more as a lifestyle.

After LeMond won his first tour, he crashed on a training ride
and broke his wrist. While recovering from the wrist injury, he went
out turkey hunting, was accidentally shot, and nearly died.

Three years later, with thirty-five shotgun pellets still in his
body, he came back and won the Tour de France in 1989 and 1990.
After he rode the fastest time trial in the history of the Tour de
France, his '89 victory was won by just eight seconds, winning the
race by the narrowest margin in history.

We hit Yankton just as Steve Miller was letting us know that
"Time keeps on slippin', slippin', slippin'… into the future."

US-81 narrowed to one lane due to road construction. I was
happy not to be on my bike. This reprieve allowed me to put this

bike trip into perspective. It wasn't just a bike trip. It was an adventure, and adventures were not dictated by the expected. They were adventures because of the unexpected things that happened and how we embraced the challenges.

The Choose Your Own Adventure book series was created in 1979. I devoured these books, it helped that they had more illustrations than words. The reader was presented with options and those options sometimes ended favorably and sometimes less so. In some cases, the story ended most disturbingly, especially for a nine-year-old.

In the book *Inside UFO 54-40*, one of your fates was described as follows:

"The hours stretch into days; the days stretch into weeks. Now you have waited so long that the computer tells you your chances of surviving hibernation are nearly zero. You can only hope that somehow your crystal ship will reach the new planet before you grow old and die, or that you will at last find the Aloha, or that something will happen to fix the ship's hyper time device. But the months go by and nothing changes. You grow more and more depressed as you sit and wait, and finally, disoriented by the incredible loneliness of outer space, you lose all will to survive. The End."

That was pretty heavy shit for a kid.

This 1970-something four-door Pontiac LeMans, sans muffler, was my crystal ship—not in the same way Jim Morrison sang about a crystal ship, which many believed represented a drug trip. No, this Pontiac LeMans crystal ship was leading me away from my self-loathing. It re-oriented me, my ibogaine.[17]

We crossed the Missouri River, and just like that, we were in Nebraska.

Fifty-eight miles later, we were cruising down Johnny Carson Boulevard through Norfolk. Johnny was born in Iowa but moved to Norfolk as a kid, where the people named a boulevard after him as well as Norfolk's Johnny Carson Theater. We passed by his childhood home at 306 South Thirteenth Street and motored out of town.

My chauffeur was finishing his third joint when we arrived in Columbus. Even with the windows down, I was pretty stoned, which had me in a very tranquil space.

"I'll get out here," I said. "By the way, what's your name?"

"Mike," he told me. "Thanks for being cool, man."

In Columbus, I fixed my flat in front of the Dairy Queen, put my bike back together, denied myself a Peanut Buster Parfait, and moved on.

It was probably around two in the afternoon, hot with no wind.

South of town, a full-sized Higgins boat with three bronze GIs storming a beach sat just before the bridge over the Loup River. The abbreviation GI stood for "Government Issue" and generically referred to the US Army soldier. The sand beneath the memorial was collected from all the beaches across the globe where Higgins boats carried soldiers ashore, including the D-Day beaches at Normandy.

---

17 A psychoactive substance found in plants which is used in the reduction or elimination of addiction to opioids.

"Andrew Higgins," Eisenhower said, "is the man who won the war for us. If Higgins had not designed and built those LCVPs, we never could have landed over an open beach. The whole strategy of the war would have been different."

It was rumored that Higgins built his first boat in the basement of his home, despite the small detail of having to remove it from the basement at some point. He eventually knocked down a wall to get his boat to the water. I could see myself doing that very thing. That was if I had any patience or knew how to build a boat.

We had an LCM-8—Landing Craft Mechanized, Mark 8—on Wake Island. It was an evolution of the Higgins Boat. We took it out to deep-sea fish a couple of Sundays. It was loud, belched out a tremendous amount of black diesel exhaust, and was terribly slow. We would load it up with beers and troll around the island, catching a buzz and a few Ono,[18] which I learned very quickly to be an extremely tasty fish.

I sprinted over the shoulder-less, rusty girder bridge crossing the Loup River.

Grand Island was sixty-six miles away. I smiled, not because I had only sixty-six miles to go, but also because I was pretty stoned. The texture of the air was smooth and silky as it wrapped itself around me. The sun drew me forward, its heat magnetically pulled me west. Cycling was effortless. I should have asked Mike for some weed to go, to help make the rest of Nebraska "fly" by.

---

18 Hawaiian word meaning "good to eat." It is commonly known as wahoo and is a close relative of the king mackerel.

I passed Duncan, then Silver Creek eleven miles later.

I was kicking out an average speed of nineteen miles per hour. The eight gods were blowing the wind in my favor now.

Another eleven miles and I was in Clarks; ten more and I arrived in Central City.

Almost one hundred years prior to my arrival, notices were posted around Central City, similar to this:

Homes For Children
═══ WANTED ═══

A Company of Homeless Children from the East Will Arrive at

McPherson, Friday, September 15.

These children are of various ages and of both sexes, having been thrown friendless upon the world. They come under the auspices of the Children's Aid Society, of New York. They are well disciplined, having come from various orphanages. The citizens of this community are asked to assist the agent in finding good homes for them. Persons taking these children must be recommended by the local committee. They must treat the children in every way as members of the family, sending them to school, church, Sabbath school and properly clothe them until they are 18 years old. Protestant children placed in Protestant homes and Catholic children in Catholic homes. The following well known citizens have agreed to act as a local committee to aid the agents in securing homes:

Dr. Heaston	H. A. Rowland	C. W. Bachelor
F. A. Vaniman	W. J. Krehbiel	K. Sorensen

Applications must be made to and endorsed by the local committee.

An address will be given by the agents. Come and see the children and hear the address. Distribution will take place at

Opera House, Friday, September 15

at 10:00 a. m. and 2:00 p. m.

Notices like this were handed out to announce the arrival of an Orphan Train.

The signs read:

```
┌─────────────────────────────────────┐
│                                      │
│          WANTED                      │
│                                      │
│    HOMES FOR ORPHAN CHILDREN         │
│                                      │
│      A COMPANY OF ORPHAN             │
│     CHILDREN, UNDER THE              │
│        AUSPICES OF THE               │
│     CHILDREN'S AID SOCIETY           │
│          OF NEW YORK                 │
│                                      │
│           WILL BE IN                 │
│    CENTRAL CITY, NOVEMBER 11         │
│                                      │
└─────────────────────────────────────┘
```

The sign continued... These children are of various ages and of both sexes, having been thrown friendless upon the world. They come under the auspices of the Children's Aid Society of New York. They are well disciplined, having come from various orphanages. The citizens of this community are asked to assist the agent in finding good homes for them. Persons taking these children must be recommended by the local committee. They must greet the children in every way as members of the family, sending them to school, church, Sabbath school and properly clothe them until they are 18 years old. Protestant children placed in Protestant homes and Catholic children in Catholic homes.

During what became the largest migration of children in the world, orphan trains relocated almost a quarter of a million homeless and orphaned kids from the big cities in the Northeast to the Midwest between 1854 and 1929.

When I was nine years old, I remember watching the made-for-TV movie, *Orphan Train*. It starred Glenn Close and Melissa Michaelsen, who was my first ever TV crush—well, maybe my second. Jo Polniaczek on *The Facts of Life*, played by Nancy McKeon, wasn't all that hard on the eyes, but way out of my league. I had a chance with Melissa… or so I thought.

Orphan Train made my head spin as a kid. I wanted to climb into the TV and join their saga. I dismissed the fact that these kids were without homes and families and probably starving. Instead, I envied their adventure. Their independence. Wandering the tracks, begging for scraps. The hobo life in search of stability, whereas I had stability and was in search of the hobo life—one with Melissa Michaelsen.

Just outside of Central City, I stopped and stared north, scanning the Great Plains. Once wild, now tamed and trapped, surgically sliced up into squares and scratched with furrows—vast, magical, empty. It was eerily quiet. Geese flapped south in a V-formation.

Ever wonder, when you saw a flock of geese, why one side of the V was longer than the other? I'll tell you, it was because there were more geese on that side.

In the same fashion Mike arrived in my life, a 1990s Honda Civic pulled up behind me unannounced. It was a four-door hatchback with a generous amount of rust.

Two guys got out and asked me if I wanted a ride.

"I'm just going sixteen more miles to Grand Island."

"So are we."

"Well, okay!"

I was in a good mood, still a little stoned. What possibly could go wrong?

They popped the hatchback and slid in my bike and pack. Once in the backseat, I realized the rear window and both back windows were not tinted but were, in fact, spray-painted black. I couldn't see out except for through the front windshield. In the back seat of that Honda, I didn't exist to the outside world.

Then there were the back doors. After shutting the door, I realized they could only be opened from the outside. An experience not unfamiliar to me for the few times I had found myself in the back of a police car.

As the car left the shoulder, I felt us crossing over the rumble strips and realized that this was a really stupid idea. Certainly not my first.

◎

In 1998, I found myself in Havana, Cuba.

I was on the tail end of a month-long trip that started with running the Disney World Marathon in Florida. I then flew to Panama City, Panama. With a backpack, passport, and five hundred dollars cash, I worked my way up through Panama, Costa Rica, Honduras, El Salvador, Nicaragua, and finally ended up in a hostel on Isla Mujeres just off the coast of Cancún, Mexico, over four weeks.

My next scheduled stop was going to be New Orleans. I was registered to run the Mardi Gras Marathon and then take the Amtrak back to Minneapolis. I had never taken the Amtrak cross-country and thought it would be a great way to recover from two marathons and one month of backpacking.

Cuba wasn't on my radar until a Swedish girl stood up after a few drinks and shouted, "Who wants to go to Cuba with me?"

Your hero, who was also a few drinks in, responded in the affirmative. Twelve hours later, we were in Cuba.

Ernest Hemingway wrote, "*Mi mojito in La Bodeguita, mi daiquiri en El Floridita*."

Our first night in Havana, we found La Bodeguita and El Floridita and partook in many of Hemingway's favorites.

Me and the Swede in Cuba

Later that night, we were arm in arm, stumbling along the Malecón, when two guys offered to give us a ride to our hotel for five dollars.

We agreed and fell into the backseat of the unmarked taxi. My Swedish companion referred to it as a *svarttaxi*—"black taxi."

Soon realizing we probably hadn't put ourselves in the best situation, I told my Swedish companion to be ready to jump out if shit got real. It was more tough talk than anything, but if the car did come to a stop, we agreed to kick the door open and jump out.

In the end, it all worked out. We made it to the hotel and celebrated our adventure with another mojito and a couple of cigars, hand-rolled by a seventy-year-old woman in the lobby. A week later, I completed the Mardi Gras Marathon.

I told myself I wouldn't do something stupid like that again. *Something stupid* like getting into a shitty white four-door hatchback with spray-painted windows driven by two strangers and Jesus on the dashboard, somewhere in Nebraska.

I leaned forward between the two men, both of whom were Latino. "*Dónde está?*"

The driver was about fifty and the passenger was in his late twenties.

"*México. Mi amigo es esta Honduras,*" the driver replied.

"*Pardon, por favor, no mucho habla español.*" I probably sounded like a kindergartner.

The driver looked at me in the rearview mirror and smiled. "I speak English. Fernando does not."

"I'm Cory."

"I'm Wilfredo." Wilfredo told me they were working the harvest, making money to send back home to help support their families.

I leaned back and stared at the spray-painted windows. I started to scratch the one to my right with my fingernail. This Honda Civic was my Château d'If.[19]

Wilfredo looked in the rearview mirror and shared with me his concern that the world was in its last days. The second coming of Christ was going to happen very soon.

He told me about the time he was born again at a tent revival just outside Wichita, Kansas. There was a man there, who, according to Wilfredo, had one eye. His other eye was completely gone—just an empty socket.

"It's a miracle," Wilfredo exclaimed. "If you cover his good eye, he can see out of the socket."

"He can see out of his socket, with no eye?"

"Yes, you can go there yourself and meet him. He is in Wichita."

"So, you're telling me there's a guy in Wichita who can see out of his eye socket?"

"Yes, it's a miracle!"

"Clearly. And they danced with vipers and drank strychnine, did they?"

The car slowed down, and we turned into a dirt lot full of trailer homes.

"Is this Grand Island?"

19 Prison in Alexandre Dumas's *The Count of Monte Cristo*.

On the map, Grand Island looked like it might have buildings, gas stations, maybe a Taco Bell—preferably a Subway. I was going through mayonnaise withdrawal. All I saw were a few trailer homes and an abnormal number of broken-down vehicles.

"It's about five miles down the road."

He parked the car in front of the third trailer. "Come in. You are hungry."

Was I hungry? I didn't think so. But if there was a cold beer in the fridge, I'd certainly take it off his hands.

We all got out of the car. I left my bike in the back along with my pack and my common sense. I was seriously questioning my situation. But hey, let's see how far we could go down this rabbit hole.

Entering the trailer home, a rather large white woman with a faded heart tattoo on her forearm was wearing a muumuu, sweating over a stove, frying up dinner. The trailer home smelled like hamburger and onions. The faux-oak furniture matched the wood paneling and brown and green shag carpeting, which did an excellent job hiding any dirt and/or stains that may have resided in its weaves.

When she saw me, the woman didn't appear to be surprised. I guess Wilfredo brought home more than one stranger.

Maybe she was cooking up the last one Wilfredo brought home. The furniture appeared to be store-bought and not part of the Ed Gein[20] collection. Wilfredo offered me a seat, pointing to the flower-patterned loveseat.

---

20 Nicknamed the Butcher of Plainfield, Ed made furniture using exhumed corpses and his murdered victims, along with other 'trophies' using their skin and bones.

I was still stoned.

Wilfredo introduced me to his wife and handed me a bible. Fernando kissed Wilfredo's wife on the cheek and sat in a worn-out recliner in the corner of the living room.

Fernando stared at me like a protective guard dog, ready to pounce if I gave off a hint of aggression.

I stared back until Wilfredo's wife dropped a glass on the floor, which startled both of us and broke our stares.

My focus was now on her. She fussed with the skillet. How many bad decisions did she have to make to end up here? Maybe she was happy wearing her muumuu and cooking fried things. Sex with Wilfredo could very well have been mind-blowing. Maybe she was once an executive at 3M who said screw it and opted to live this simple life, reading *Reader's Digest*, watching reruns of *Gilligan's Island*, drinking Boone's Farm, and yelling at the neighbors for letting their dog shit on her patch of dirt. She was curious, but not interesting.

Wilfredo stood between me and the muumuu and assigned me some selected passages he wanted to share. He was determined to save a soul this day, but my soul was tired and wanted to be in Grand Island, not in a trailer home on the outskirts of town. To make things worse, they had no beer.

He sat down in his chair. "I want to share with you some verses. Go to Acts 2:38."[21]

---

21 Peter replied, "Repent and be baptized, every one of you, in the name of Jesus Christ for the forgiveness of your sins. And you will receive the gift of the Holy Spirit."

He spoke to me as if I was his student and him, my teacher. I found Acts 2:38 quickly, while Wilfredo struggled in his search, lost somewhere in Psalms.

"It's in the New Testament," I said.

He continued to flip through the bible, frazzled.

"You're in the Old Testament. Acts is in the New Testament. Mathew, Mark, Luke, John, ACTS!"

He kept flipping pages.

"NEW TESTAMENT!" I said loudly.

He shut his bible and looked at me frustrated, "You already believe in God? You know the bible very well."

"I wouldn't say I know the bible at all, really. I just had to memorize the books of the bible when I was a kid. My parents sent me to a Christian academy, grades five through seven, and apparently, it stuck. Sort of like memorizing the presidents of the US with a song."

I broke into melody, "There was Washington, Adams, and then Thomas Jefferson. Madison, Monroe, and John Quincy Adams."

Wilfredo stared at me.

"Just songs I remember that I learned as a kid. Never thought they would be useful in life. Apparently, I was wrong."

"Would you like to stay for dinner?"

I thought about the rareness of this opportunity. When would I ever have the chance to have an authentic, trailer-home dinner in the middle of Nebraska with a Mexican, Honduran, and a large woman in a muumuu?

I was sure I'd never have an offer like that again, but I could see the sun setting. There were still five miles to get to Grand Island.

"No thank you, I need to get to Grand Island before it gets dark. I don't have lights for my bike."

I stood up, put the bible on the couch, and made for the door. Wilfredo stood up, blocking me from the door, and again offered me dinner.

Things became uncomfortable—the bulldog, Fernando, stood up in a very aggressive way. There was no doubt in my mind Fernando would win whatever physical altercation might have arisen.

I smiled and worked my way around Wilfredo.

"I need to get my bike and pack out of your car."

We walked outside, and he opened the hatchback. I scanned the area looking for a place to run if the situation required it, but I was wearing my cycling shoes. Speed would not have been on my side.

"That looks like a very expensive bike, my friend."

Wilfredo was to my right; Fernando came out and stood to my left. Both watched me slip on my front wheel and tighten the quick release. Fernando looked up at Wilfredo but didn't speak. I anticipated that very soon, a blunt object would crush my skull.

Pretending all was right with the world, I searched for my happy place, while simultaneously preparing myself to be taken out and everything stolen from me.

What if this was it for me, Cory's Last Stand. Right here in a dirt parking lot surrounded by trailer homes off Route 30. A historic marker in memory of me would be placed feet from where I stood.

I wondered if I would know I was dead. Is there an afterlife, heaven, purgatory, hell, nirvana, reincarnation? Will my body become twenty-one grams lighter after my soul leaves my body as Duncan MacDougall[22] hypothesized? Will they throw me in a ditch, my final purpose as a food source for scavengers?

Did we roam the planet as spirits when we died? Spend eternity haunting houses, bars, bridges, and back roads? When Grandpa Mortensen died, Grandma complained about Grandpa's active presence in their house.

"Even now, after he's dead, he still won't leave me alone," she once told me.

Maybe I would become a story on Art Bell's *Coast to Coast*. "The Legend of the Grand Island Cyclist." I'd haunt this stretch of Route 30. People would tell stories of how they stopped to help a cyclist with a flat tyre on the side of the road, and as they drove off, they would look into their rearview mirror, only to find I had vanished.

"Mmm, no," I said. "Not really. It's probably worth about a hundred bucks. It's old and all scratched up."

He didn't believe me. I didn't care. My bike was worth six months of trailer payments.

"Are you sure you don't want to stay?"

I didn't answer.

Mounting my aluminum steed, I ticked off a salute, crossed Route 30, and pedaled toward Grand Island, hoping with all

---

22 MacDougall attempted to prove the soul had a physical weight. While using six patients at the moment of death, it turned out one of the six subjects lost three-fourths of an ounce (21.3 grams) at the time of death, concluding the test.

thirty-seven trillion cells in my body that they would just go back into their trailer and forget about yours truly. Which apparently, they did.

I was free. Free from Wilfredo and Fernando, free from the Greyhound idea, free from quitting, free to move forward—at my pace, on my time. My only limitation was the road.

No matter how free you thought you were, the road was limiting. The road allowed me to travel along its spine. My destination predetermined by some engineers and construction crews who were no longer alive. All things were preordained. I was a cyclist following a line on a map toward a city of immature lights.

French fur traders originally called this place *La Grande Isle*. In 1857, a group of German immigrants moved in with the *grand* idea of relocating Washington, DC, to Grand Island due to its central location in the future United States, even though Nebraska wasn't even a state in 1857. I applauded their forward-thinking, but it never happened. That did not stop Grand Island from becoming a capital city. In the 1990s, it was considered the meth capital of Nebraska—a far less glorious achievement but one, nonetheless.

Route 30 turned into Second Street, and my options looked bleak with regards to finding a motel.

Catty-corner of Pioneer Park was a Pump & Pantry. I stopped in and asked if there was a place to camp. The girl behind the counter told me about six miles south of town, just off I-80, was a place called Mormon Island State Recreation Area that offered camping.

It was almost dark, and my previous oneness with the world and all the Zen bullshit of cycling along the lines of unified cosmic blah-blahness had begun to wane.

I was pissed that I had to ride another thirty minutes to get to this campsite, thus adding six miles to tomorrow's ride. Plus, what would I do if, when I got to the Mormon Island State Recreation Area, they had no camping available? My finding a place to sleep tonight was predicated entirely on a nineteen-year-old girl working at a Pump & Pantry who had probably never even been to Mormon Island State Recreation Area.

I could see high-speed lights from the vehicles heading east and west on I-80. The distance that those vehicles covered in ten minutes took me an hour. It took the pioneers in a covered wagon all day, so what was I complaining about.

Before the highway, I saw the glow of the Bosselman Travel Center.

It was two stories high with seemingly hundreds of semi-trailers parked around it. The sound of diesel engines idling and hydraulic brakes releasing joined the orchestra of crickets and frogs surrounding the compound.

Inside, one could find discounted flannel shirts, endless supplies of beef jerky and porn, and electronics for every purpose. Then there was the life-size statue of the Predator, the alien creature from Hollywood's *Predator* franchise. God only knew why that was there—well, God and the owner of the Bosselman.

With a pizza from Little Caesars, I sat outside on the curb next to my bike, thinking of a way to hit up a trucker for a ride west. I was sweaty, salty, smelly, and wearing Lycra—I had all the makings of a male lot lizard, only with a bike.

I was no longer pissed about the six extra miles, the question was, "Do I ride, or do I hitch?"

After the day's two hitches, it could go either way. Your hero would have a new tale to tell about his westward adventure. Only the arrival date would change. Or maybe I'd end up in a cult. Who could say, really? I took a bite of my pizza and stared at my legs. They were filthy.

Mormon Island was one mile south of the Bosselman. After filling up on the pizza and having not totally sold myself on another hitch, I grabbed my bike and pedaled across the Platte River, where I exchanged ten dollars for a campsite.

Two campsites down was a guy grooming a horse. I set up my tent and introduced myself.

"Where is your trailer?"

"No trailer. I'm riding across the United States."

"On a horse?"

"Yep." He pointed at my bike. "You look like you're riding too."

"Yeah, but a horse?"

He made his way to the other side of the horse and stopped talking. I didn't get horse people.

I crawled into my tent and finally called it a day, with the sound of the traffic from I-80 as my lullaby.

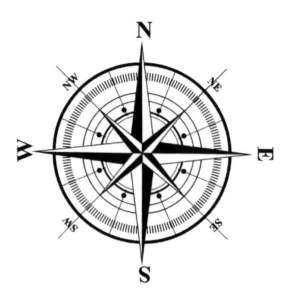

CHAPTER 5

DAY FIVE

AUGUST 26, 2001

Today's Ride: Grand Island, Nebraska - Gothenburg, Nebraska
Today's Distance: 99 Miles

A small platoon of mosquitoes rested on the fragile mesh screen which prevented them from feasting on our hero.

Like bees, it was only the female mosquito that bit, or, in the case of the bee, stung. The female praying mantis devoured the male after mating, as did the female octopus. Often, the male sacrificed himself to the female to provide her with the much-needed protein for her to recover and to ensure the survival of their offspring. Let's celebrate this evolutionary accomplishment of female domination.

I stared at the mosquitoes. They stared at me, with the hundreds of lenses in their little eyes. Hatching a plan to penetrate the mesh and find their way to a buffet of blood.

I hit the tent. The mosquitoes flew away, then returned. This process repeated several times until the sun hit the tent, and, like vampires, they scattered to darker corners.

After the last few drops of dew melted away, I packed up the tent and rolled up the air mattress.

My air mattress was only a half-inch thick when inflated, but it was better than sleeping on the ground. It protected me from the cold wet earth and random pebbles or branches hiding under my tent.

Even so, sleeping on it was anything but comfortable. Ten minutes of stretching was required before the aches and pains dissipated and I felt normal enough to ride again.

How would I pack for today's ride? Would it be the same as yesterday, or would I experiment—put the sleeping bag in first rather than second? What great difference would the changes make?

I thought about where I started and how I got to where I was. What would the day have in store for me, aside from cornfields and distant trains, which were pretty much a guarantee?

I pedaled over to a diner just down the road, locked up my bike, and moseyed on in.

Out west, people *moseyed.* The Americanism had no known origin.

During our brief existence, we US Americans had created many words and phrases, many of which made no sense to those from outside our borders—often, they didn't make sense for some of us inside.

Catch-22,[23] *bee's knees,*[24] *behind the eight ball,*[25] and *on the war path*[26]—possibly even the phrase *go west* might fall into that

---

23 A problematic situation for which the only solution is denied by a circumstance inherent in the problem.
24 Excellent or very high quality.
25 In a bad situation, in a losing position.
26 Angry, miffed. Ready for a fight.

category. Did they say, "Go west, young man," in France, Burma, or New Zealand?

The phrase *out west* conjured up certain cultural images. Nebraska was certainly part of it, though it might not be the state that people thought of when they thought of the American West.

The fact was that on the banks of the Old Man River[27] in Missouri stood the St. Louis Arch. The actual name was Jefferson National Expansion Memorial designed by Eero Saarinen,[28] dedicated to the US American people in honor of their westward expansion. One could say everything west of the Mississippi River was *out west.*

It conjured up images of deserts, mountains, rattlesnakes, canyons, Gila monsters, Native Americans, the smell of campfire, and sage. Jeremiah Johnson, Billy the Kid, refried beans, stagecoaches, rodeos, gun fights at noon, saloons serving whiskey for breakfast, and brothels. Hangings, rustlers, teepees, pow wows, and a lonely cowboy making music with his harmonica near a dying fire.

The West had a romantic mystique, but it was a hard, barren, and unforgiving place.

Out west was where you'd find, in my opinion, the best sausage gravy in the world. It'd clog your arteries faster than lighting. The thicker, chunkier, and spicier the gravy, the better. And the biscuits, if you so chose to enjoy, must be deep, heavy, shiny, and doughy, not flaky.

27 One of many nicknames of the Mississippi River.
28 Finnish architect known for his neo-futuristic designs.

Oh, those from Tennessee or Georgia might disagree, but I'd had sausage gravy in all of these here United States, and the Southwest had the best. All invitations to prove me wrong would be accepted.

I sat at the counter and ordered two eggs—sunny side up, hash browns—crispy, toast—white, and a cup of sausage gravy. I mixed it all together in a sloppy mess and shoveled it down with the help of one of the four triangle pieces of toast that accompanied the meal.

As I was enjoying my breakfast, a gentleman—perhaps thirty years my senior—sat down next to me.

"Where you off to?" he asked while staring at the empty coffee cup in front of him. The waitress was prompt in filling it.

"Heading west. California," I said while simultaneously shoveling in my breakfast.

"That's great," the man said. "It's good to see people traveling. You have to do it while you're still young and not married." He took a sip of his coffee. "Did you just finish school, then?"

"No," I answered. "Well, yeah, I guess. I finished school eight years ago."

The question threw me. I had just survived two dubious hitch-hikings, won a battle (maybe more of a siege) against a platoon of mosquitoes, and had a warm plate of cholesterol that was only half-eaten. I was not in the mood for this inquisition.

Truth be told, I never finished college. I decided I was finished with college after two years of university with nothing to show for it but four thousand dollars in student loan debt.

Still, I talked with the man for ten more minutes—small talk about unimportant things like the weather. The conversation was a hair more interesting than listening to the farm reports piping out of the diner speakers:

Corn: Steady to down one

Soybeans: Down two to four

Wheat: Steady to down two

Grain futures are mixed this morning, reversing patterns from a wild day in many markets on Tuesday.

Markets got caught up with those losses in Asia today but turned higher in Europe, with US index futures pointing towards a rebound today.

In my twenties, I would take a lot of road trips on my 1980 BMW R65 motorcycle. Mostly just to explore the backroads. I'd be gone for weeks. Sometimes, I'd challenge myself to see how far I could go without sleeping. Typically, I started hallucinating after thirty-six hours of being awake.

The worst hallucination was during a trip west. My buddy Adam and I left Minneapolis after a full workday. We drove straight to Sturgis, South Dakota, a nine-hour drive on the R65. We spent the day in Sturgis and drove straight back that evening. A storm came through, which helped keep us awake, but as I was driving down a street near my home that night, I came across a woman with no skin laying in the middle of the street unable to stand. Her body bobbed up and down as she attempted to hold herself up with one arm and reached for me with the other. I went into a full panic and drove past. Gathering my nerve, I turned back to confirm what I saw. It turned out that a large branch had broken off a tree and ended up in the street, the wind rustling its branches.

My dad drove his motorcycle from Minneapolis to Phoenix in thirty-six hours, straight through. I tried beating that record once and got as far as Tucumcari, New Mexico. My motorcycle did sixty-five miles per hour with a tailwind, whereas my dad's was geared for the autobahn and could do one-twenty-five in fourth gear. I knew because I did it once. Still had one more gear to go if I had wanted to really open it up.

The farm report was one of the most reliable AM stations you could find. Once, when trying to dial in an AM station, I came across Art Bell's *Coast to Coast*. The show became a late-night staple in my life. I would listen to it driving in the early morning and, if I was pulling an all-nighter at the office trying to meet a deadline, he'd keep me company.

Art Bell was all about the paranormal, government conspiracies, ghosts, and aliens. Those who called in or were guests of the show all claimed to have seen ghosts, been abducted by aliens, or thought they were an alien.

One show I recalled, Art opened up a phone line and invited people who thought they were the antichrist to dial in.

"Hey Art. I'm the antichrist. Long time listener, first time caller."

Art brought out the people who hid in the shadows of society, living off the grid, and welcomed them into his safe, on-air space. Like a mysterious unknown grandfather, he embraced them, respected their beliefs and theories, gave them a voice and a place to commune, even if it was just for three hours a night.

Some of his guests were former government workers who claimed to be part of big conspiracies and "confirmed" the existence of things like:

- Area 51
- The US government assassination of Martin Luther King, Jr.
- Contrails (chemtrails) poisoning Americans
- The CIA invented AIDS to wipe out gay and black communities
- FDR knew about the attack on Pearl Harbor before it happened
- The lunar landing was faked

There were endless conversations about the New World Order, Bilderberg Group, the World Bank, the Illuminati, and Bohemian Grove.

Creatures entered the mix with frequency—Chupacabra, the Jersey Devil, Mothman, and one I was familiar with from when I was a Boy Scout at Camp Geronimo, sitting around the fire—the Mogollon Monster.

As the campfire story about the Mogollon Monster was told to us, a man by the name of Sam Spade built a cabin not too far from Camp Geronimo back in the 1900s. Sam was attacked by the Mogollon Monster, the bigfoot of Arizona, but managed to fight it off. The episode tormented him the rest of his life. The creature came back on the day his son, Bill Spade, married and killed Bill and his new wife.

The storyteller finished by saying that the creature still lurked in the woods in search of its next victim. Then, we were all sent back to our tents, which required us to walk a few hundred yards in the darkness, scared out of our wits.

For his listeners, Art Bell opened the door to possibility. I couldn't say there were or weren't aliens or Chupacabra, or if the Mogollon Monster still lurked in the woods around Camp Geronimo. I did believe we landed on the moon. I didn't think for a moment chemtrails were poisoning us. I did think there were some crazy shenanigans going on out there at Area 51. Although Area 52 was where the true craziness was.

Just kidding, there was no Area 52.

Or was there?

With a pound of eggs, hash browns, toast, and gravy settling in my belly, I thought I could make North Platte, a mere 146 miles away. I'd never ridden that far in one day, but I didn't really think my goal through.

My Rand McNally map of Nebraska showed that I could save myself from backtracking the six miles north by cutting west on Guenther Road, hooking up with Route 30 just west of Alda.

Guenther Road was a bumpy road laden with obstacles like mud, loose gravel, and corn husks.

Once on Route 30, I started out at a solid eighteen-mile-per-hour pace with the help of a tailwind.

I could do this. I could get to North Platte, no problem. Eighteen miles per hour equaled 180 miles in ten hours. I only had to go 140 miles—seven hours and forty-seven minutes. I could be there by dinner.

Out along the empty shoulder, while continuing to chase a vanishing point that I would never catch, my math skills sharpened.

Wood River to Shelton was eight miles. At eighteen miles per hour, I would arrive in Shelton in twenty-six minutes.

To pass the time, I experimented with different speeds. If I kicked it up a notch and averaged nineteen miles per hour, I'd be in Shelton in twenty-five minutes. From Wood River to North Platte was 122 miles. If I biked an average pace of sixteen miles per hour, I would be in North Platte in seven hours thirty-seven minutes.

It was all just numbers. The wind was a number; the sun was a number; the friction of my tyres rolling along the bituminous was a number. My gears were numbers. A fifty-tooth ring in the front and a twenty-two in the back created a ratio.

The incline and decline of the road were numbers. I was surrounded by numbers. My entire being was numbers.

I broke up the ride into another number—four.

1. The Great Plains
2. The Rocky Mountains
3. The Southwest Desert
4. The Sierra Nevadas

Then, there were the numbers within the numbers. The numbers of the day, the hour, my speed, calories burned, temperature. Every second, a number represented an opportunity missed.

I was about twelve miles outside of Kearney, Nebraska when my rear tube blew. This time, it was a bit more than just a tube. My tyre had actually torn about a half-inch. The tear was the result of my brake pad rubbing against the tyre. At some point, I must have bumped the brake pad just enough to knock it out of alignment, probably when I was pulling it out of the back of Wilfredo's car.

There was a trick to resolve the torn tyre issue while out on a ride. You took a dollar bill, assuming you had one—any denomination would do—and folded it a few times to cover the tear in the tyre. This would allow you to insert a new tube without it popping out of the tyre where the tear was, allowing you to get home or, in my case, to the next bike shop.

I didn't learn this trick until a few years after my ride to California when I cycled from Los Angeles to San Diego.

So, in Nebraska, I found myself walking along the shoulder, definitely not going to reach North Platte for dinner.

With my thumb extended, I walked for about fifteen minutes until a white, windowless van stopped just ahead of me. Shit, the two CIA agents from the field in Minnesota finally caught me.

Instead, a heavyset, jovial, young guy—about twenty-five—got out of the van. "Have some trouble?"

"Yeah, I tore my tyre. Need to find a bike shop."

"There's one in Kearney, just ten minutes ahead," he said while opening the back of the van. "I can take you there. I'm headed to Kearney."

We loaded the bike.

"I wouldn't have picked you up if you didn't have the bike. I figured something was wrong, that's why I stopped."

"Well, I appreciate that."

"I picked up a guy six weeks ago. He pulled a knife on me. I ended up stopping and getting the police's attention. They arrested him and found LSD and pot on him. I told myself, that's the last time I pick up a hitchhiker, but you had your bike, so I figured I'd help out."

"Well, thanks again." I reached over and shook his hand. "Name's Cory."

"I'm Andy."

"What do you do?"

"I sell and fix printers. I'm delivering that printer right now." He pointed to the back of the van. "That back there costs six thousand dollars."

I didn't even turn around.

"Hey! Have you seen the Archway Monument?"

"No! What's the Archway Monument?" I assumed it was some sort of natural wonder.

"You've never heard of the Archway Monument? It's been in a movie with Jack Nicholson even! Movie was called *Schmidt*, or *About Schmidt*. Has Kathy Bates in it. She's even naked!"

He looked over with a *shit-eating grin* (another Americanism).

While I liked Kathy Bates and thought she was an amazing actress, the thought of her naked didn't do much in the way of arousing me. When I thought about her, I always thought about that hobbling scene in *Misery* and shuddered.

"Nope, never heard of the Archway Monument, or that movie. So, what is this monument?"

"It's a bridge across I-80 with restaurants and stuff in it, you can almost see it from Kearney. President Bill Clinton visited after it opened even."

I was neither interested in nor impressed by this monument, and I wondered why he finished his sentences with the word "even." Andy was excited about it, and he was my ride to the bike shop, so I shared in his enthusiasm and told him I really looked forward to checking it out after I got a new tyre.

"So, do you live in Kearney?" I asked.

"No, Grand Island."

"Like it?"

"No, I hate it. I hate living in Grand Island!"

"Why do you stay?"

"My wife's family lives there, and she doesn't want to move."

"You're married!"

I was surprised. He looked so young.

"Yep, and I have five kids even."

"FIVE KIDS? Jesus, I can't even imagine taking care of a dog."

He looked over and smiled.

He took me to Kearney Cycling & Fitness on Second Street. As
we drove, I noticed the library was just around the corner and down
the street. I thanked him for the ride and dragged my bike into the
shop.

"Y'all have tyres and tubes for a road bike?"

The shop was small and contained a couple of mountain bikes,
some home exercise equipment, and some miscellaneous pieces of
exercise clothing and gear. Not really a bike shop, not really a fitness
shop, but had enough of each to bear the name.

"Yes, over there," said the clerk, pointing to the far back wall.

"Here," he grabbed my bike. "Let me have a look."

He wheeled it to a back room and mounted it on a stand.

"Which tyre do you recommend? I'm riding cross-country."

"Continental Gatorskin. That's the one I use."

"Okay, let's use that one. And I'll need five tubes and some tyre
irons. Any chance I can get you to put on a new tube and the tyre?"

As he worked, I wandered around the shop, looking for anything else I might need. I added a patch kit to the pile. Fifteen minutes went by, and he rolled my bike up to the front.

"I trued your rear wheel, tightened your stem, and your brakes
needed adjusting. They were rubbing on your tyre."

"Really? That's awesome! Thanks."

"It's a bit late in the season to be biking cross-country. Most
people come through here late May, early June."

"Really? You get a lot of cross-country bikers?"

I hadn't seen one cyclist since I left Minneapolis.

"Oh yeah, this is a popular corridor for cross-country bikers. You haven't seen one? That's surprising."

He hit the register. "Twenty-nine dollars."

"Twenty-nine? You didn't add the tyre, tyre irons, patch kit, and tubes."

"No problem, you're covered. Just have a safe trip."

On my tuned-up bike, the library was a short forty-second ride. I locked up the bike against a *No Parking* sign and entered.

The librarian gave me ten minutes of internet time. There were more than thirty messages from family and friends. All short and sweet, filled with encouragement. I followed up with a single email and cc'd all. A brief message about my whereabouts. If I went missing, at least there would be a record of my last known location. My next hitch might not end as favorably as the first ones, or a car might drift onto the shoulder, the driver busy turning the dial in search of the farm report, taking your hero out.

My last breath could happen at any time.

Remember, in 2001, only about 50% of US Americans had an email account, and less than half of us had a cell phone. So, email was a relatively new form of communication. It wasn't something we woke up to and went to bed to like we do now.

We dated by meeting people at parties, through friends, at work, or through social activities.

Jobs, cars, deals on plane tickets and cruises—these were best found in the Sunday paper.

If you wanted to get online, assuming you were one of the people who had a home computer, you waited to receive the marketing CD sent in the mail from AOL, which contained three hundred free minutes of internet time. After sliding in the disk and plugging in the code, we stared at our computers, wondering what to do while each page took minutes to load. Using dial-up meant that if you had only one landline for a phone, you couldn't call out or receive calls from anyone until you were done perusing the world wide web.

I had a cell phone before leaving on my little cycling odyssey, but minutes were expensive, and service was limited. So, I canceled my plan and left my Motorola StarTAC in my kitchen junk drawer. Every hotel and motel had a phone, and I was armed with a pocketful of quarters. I had access to hundreds of payphones if I needed to make a call.

North Platte was still one hundred miles out. There was no way I was going to make it. However, there were a handful of towns along the way that might offer lodging or a city park to camp in.

With a click of the send button, I got up, thanked the librarian, unlocked my newly tuned bike, and was off, alone, heading west on a stretch of road, just outside of Kearney.

In 1957, Reinhold Schmidt also found himself alone on a stretch of road outside of Kearney, where he happened to come across a metal cylinder lying in a farm field. While checking out this mysterious piece of metal, four men and two women approached Reinhold, speaking German, which, as luck would have it, Reinhold understood.

They told him they were from Saturn and were on Earth to keep an eye on Sputnik. According to Reinhold, they had an MG convertible sports car in their spaceship so they could run errands while on Earth should they need groceries.

After a few visits with Reinhold, the Germans from Saturn took him for a ride around the Earth in their propeller-driven spacecraft. Fortunately for us, he wrote about the experience in a self-published booklet, *My Contact with the Space People.*

I would have loved to have an experience like that right about then. Only I didn't speak or understand German. My guess was the aliens would know that. I heard they were pretty clever. I based that solely on listening to all the aliens who called into Art Bell at 2:00 a.m.

"Hey, Art. Long time listener, first time caller. I'm an alien from planet LV-426."[29]

I reached Odessa in thirty minutes, population 120. Coasting through town, I wondered if anyone there had ever come across the German aliens from Saturn driving around in their little MG, picking up some milk and bread. Why would German aliens drive an MG when German engineering was far more superior? The MG was wired with Lucas Industries, such a bad electrical system that it was said Lucas held the patent on the short circuit.

Maybe the MG made sense; maybe they preferred subpar engineering? After all, their spacecraft had propellers.

---

29 From the movie *Alien*, a moon thirty-nine lightyears away from earth where 158 colonists were based.

Pedaling past Elm Creek and Overton, I arrived in Lexington, foregoing the Fill-N-Chill convenience store for a blessed Subway.

I was the only customer and made my usual order: "Footlong Spicy Italian, extra mayo."

The manager couldn't help but notice I was biking.

"Hey, care for a Gatorade? Free."

"No, that's all right."

"Look, I bike too. Here, take the Gatorade. And how about a couple of cookies? You need to eat on the road."

He charged me three dollars for everything.

Belly full of white bread, cold cuts, and mayonnaise, I walked outside into a furnace. Had to be one hundred degrees. A barely perceptible wind was coming from the east. The cicadas were deafening. The road was empty and stretched west without any possibility of ending.

John Cozad established Cozad, Nebraska, because of its location, the 100th Meridian. He also established Cozaddale back in Ohio.

John was convinced that the town would boom, as the Transcontinental Railroad headed west. A couple of things didn't go his way. The railway passed by miles south, missing the newly established town. Drought and grasshoppers plagued the few residents who lived there.

The town survived entirely because of John's incredible skill at gambling. He invested all his winnings in Cozad.

John's temper got the best of him, and he shot one of the locals over a dispute. John took his family from his namesake town, moved to Denver, and changed his name to Richard Henry Lee, never to return to Cozad—or Cozaddale, for that matter. His son, Robert Henri, would become a great artist and leader of the American Realist art movement.

It was hot, but I had a tailwind and was kicking out an average of twenty miles per hour after leaving Kearney. If it wasn't for the heat, I'd probably have kept on going to North Platte. It was one thing to say, "It's just another sixty-four miles." It was an entirely different thing to bike those sixty-four miles. Just like it was one thing to say, "I'm going to bike to California," and an entirely different thing to actually do it.

There were two Gothenburg's in the world. One was the second-largest city in Sweden, home to Volvo. The other Gothenburg could be found in Nebraska, just past the 100th meridian. Founded by Olof Bergstrom in 1882, this Gothenburg was home to 3,600 people.

Unlike John Cozad, Olof Bergstrom was such a popular person that after he was acquitted of killing Ernest Edholm in 1890, the Gothenburg Silver Cornet Band escorted him home.

I reached Gothenburg around 4:00 p.m.

Finding a motel, I entered and rang the bell. The owner emerged from behind a curtain. Through the curtain, I could see his kitchen and living room, a La-Z-Boy in front of the TV. He was chewing food as he approached the counter.

Handing me the registration card to fill out, he gulped down his mouthful.

"It's forty-two dollars for the night. Restaurant next door opens in two hours, if'n you like Mexican."

"Man, is there someplace I can get a cold beer? Like, now?"

"You just want one beer?"

"Actually, I want three beers."

"Just a second."

He disappeared behind the curtain, reappearing with a bag of four Pabst Blue Ribbon tall boys.

I could have shed a tear.

"Just take the bag. Don't tell nobody I give this to ya. Okay?"

"Yeah, I won't tell nobody. Thanks, man."

"Here's your key, room three. If you need anything else, let me know. Like I said, the restaurant next door opens at five."

It was only three o'clock. I probably could have made North Platte. But then I wouldn't be in a forty-two-dollar motel in Gothenburg with four glorious PBRs.

The first beer was gone before I made it to my room.

The room had a TV chained to the wall, a loud and agitated AC, one chair placed next to a round table, an oak-veneered nightstand, one drawer containing the Gideon Bible, and a dingy bathroom in the back.

Looking at the comforter on the bed, I cracked open the second beer. Why were motel comforters so ugly? Who came up with these patterns? Some stoned redneck reminiscing about their old Wenzel Woodsman sleeping bag with duck patterns on the inside?

When I was in Boy Scouts, this was the sleeping bag I had before upgrading to the Blue Kazoo.

The Wenzel weighed five pounds dry and thirty pounds
wet. I knew because mine got drenched on a weekend hike in the
Superstition Mountains just outside of Phoenix, and I had to carry
it eight miles out. I was also saddled with my brother's sleeping bag
after he ditched it. Our scout leader told me about the discarded
sleeping bag and instructed me—the dutiful older brother—to
go back and get it. Weren't the scouts all about personal growth?
Perhaps I became a better person because of that miserable slog.

I tore the comforter off the bed and threw it on the floor, then
drank the second beer in four big gulps. Turning the TV on for
background noise, I took a shower with my third beer.

On Wake Island, there had only been two showers for the twelve
of us in the barracks—first come, first serve. The first time I found
myself waiting in line for a shower, the guy in front of me went in
with three beers.

"What's with the beers?" I asked him.

"When I'm done with the beer, I'm done showering," he said,
cracking open the first one and slamming it. "Don't worry, it won't
be long."

After my shower, I opened the fourth beer and drank it in bed.

I never did make it to the Mexican restaurant.

CHAPTER 6

DAY SIX

AUGUST 27, 2001

Today's Ride: Gothenburg, Nebraska - Ogallala, Nebraska
Today's Distance: 87 Miles

I slept in until 8:00 a.m., then took another shower. I opened the door for some fresh air. It was clear, warm with no wind. I was checked out and on the road by eight-thirty.

As a kid, my parents had a series of books by Time Life called *The Old West*. It was a set of twenty-seven volumes about the Wild West with titles such as *The Cowboys, The Indians, The Pioneers, The Gunfighters, The Women,* and *The Great Chiefs*.

I loved these books, the myth of the Wild West captivated me. But it was the Indians that interested me most. As we learned in history class, the name Indian was given to the native people by Christopher Columbus, who mistakenly thought he had arrived in India.

The use of the word *Indian* was commonplace as a kid, but so were many words and phrases which society has now deemed insensitive or inappropriate. Personally, I found the word *inappropriate* to be inappropriate. Why not just say *wrong* or *bad* or *a real dick move*?

In the United States, American Indian was preferred over Indian, while indigenous people in Canada used First Nations. Native Americans or indigenous Americans were often used for people in both countries and Mexico.

I grew up one block from the Salt River Pima-Maricopa Indian Reservation. The reservation was created in 1879, during President Hayes's administration, under the guise of protecting the Pima and Maricopa from having their land taken away by settlers immigrating west. A bit ironic, the way it worked out.

As kids, we stole watermelons from the reservation, and in exchange, residents shot at us with BB guns loaded with salt pellets—modern-day cowboys and Indians—err Native Americans.

After WWII and the advent of air conditioning, Phoenix, AZ, the Valley of the Sun, began to grow. With that growth, the school board made two key decisions: students should be able to walk to a neighborhood elementary school and schools should have names honoring Native American traditions.

The first school to open in Scottsdale was Tavan in 1954, Kachina in 1955, Ingleside and Tonto in 1956, Kiva in 1957, Kaibab and Tonalea in 1958, and Pima, Supai, and Arcadia High School in 1959. Hohokam, Hopi, and Navajo opened in 1960. Paiute and Yavapai elementary schools opened in 1961, as did Coronado High School. Mohave opened in 1962, Cocopah and Apache opened in 1965, Saguaro High School in 1966, Pueblo in 1970, Chaparral High School in 1972, Cherokee in 1974, and Cochise in 1980.

At Pima, where I went for first through fourth grade, as well as eighth grade, we were the Pima Warriors—our mascot was an Indian warrior.

Grades nine and ten, I went to Coronado High School. We were the Coronado Dons and our mascot was a Spanish conquistador. I'm not sure how that name and mascot fit in with honoring Native American traditions.

Before Boy Scouts, I was in Indian Guides, a division of the YMCA. We were the Cherokee Tribe. I was Little Spotted Eagle. My dad was Spotted Eagle. For the most part, it was an excuse for us to pile into the car for the weekend. The dads would cook over the fire and have some adult beverages, and us boys would run around with pellet guns and wrist rockets, shooting each other in the desert at night. During the day, we tore ass on Honda ATCs[30] and dirt bikes, sans helmets or adult supervision.

Occasionally, we got together at someone's house and made crafts related to the Native Americans. Moccasins, jewelry made from beads...I recalled making a chief's headdress, though I didn't know what became of it.

As I grew older, I spent a lot of time going out on my bike and exploring the desert. Sitting alone in a dry riverbed, I tried to figure out how Native Americans made baskets using twigs, brush, and other thin strips of wood. How were they able to understand and figure out how to make pottery from the earth? Living in a dry-arid

30 Honda trademarked the term "All Terrain Cycle" and back in the 1970-80s, it was referred to as an ATC, now referred to as an ATV.

desert, surviving. Worshiping that which would kill you like the Hopi Snake Dance.

The idea of living from only that which the earth provided, whether nomadic or stationary, fascinated me. The ability to make cliff dwellings or pueblos from the earth without assistance from modern construction technology. The wisdom and knowledge to understand the science of medicine and astronomy, farming, migrations, and irrigation.

And with one order from Sir Jeffery Amherst of the British forces in North America, it all fell apart: "You will do well to try to inoculate the Indians by means of blankets, as well as to try every other method that can serve to extirpate this execrable race."

When two Indian chiefs came to a fort to ask the British to surrender, a local trader wrote in his journal: "Out of our regard for them, we gave them two Blankets and an Handkerchief out of the Small Pox Hospital. I hope it will have the desired effect."

⊙

Although I had passed a Pony Express station in Kearney, I felt rushed to get to North Platte, so I skipped visiting it, knowing there was a Pony Express station in Gothenburg. The road signs assured me of this.

I arrived just as the Gothenburg Pony Express Station opened and soon found myself in a one-room cabin, about two hundred square feet in size.

Gothenburg Pony Express Station

The isolation of these stations, the tenacity with which these people had to live and somehow survive out here, manning these little stations, really was beyond my grasp. The elements, hostile attacks, bandits, plus the loneliness had to be deafening.

I once read that one of the top causes of death in the West in those days was by self-inflicted gunshot. It was how Meriwether

Lewis, of Lewis and Clark fame, did it. Shot himself in the abdomen and head in a lodging home in the Louisiana Territory. Although there was speculation he had been murdered, Vegas odds favored suicide.

Riders willing to risk their lives to assure safe passage for a bag of mail over some of the most dangerous and desolate terrain—for twenty-five dollars a week—rode seventy-five miles a day to deliver mail from St. Joseph, Missouri, to California in just ten days. That distance took your average pioneer six months to travel in a covered wagon. It would take your hero roughly eighteen days on his trusty, still unnamed bike.

NOTE: Cost to send a letter in 1860? Five dollars. In 2019, that would be $155.00. Think about that when you complain about the price of stamps going up a few pennies.

The Pony Express lasted all of eighteen months. It never had a chance of surviving, although its place in history remains far more legendary and romantic than that of its predecessor, the telegraph.

.-- .... .- - / .... .- - .... / --. --- -.. / .-- .-. --- ..- --. .... -[31]

The town of Maxwell, Nebraska was now in my sights. It didn't offer much, but a kiosk that read *good food* reeled me in.

It was 10:00 a.m. and the last time I ate was at a Subway in Lexington, fifty miles and eighteen hours back.

I walked into the restaurant—half the place was carpeted, the other half had those linoleum squares you'd see in an elementary school… or a prison. Some were missing; some had been replaced

---

31 First telegraph in Morse code: "What hath God wrought!"

with mismatched tiles. I noticed there was no transition strip between the carpet and linoleum. Not great for my OCD.

Seating options were limited—there were seven barstools at the bar and a two-top in the middle of the room. I opted for the bar.

A woman emerged from the kitchen. She looked like life had not been kind to her.

"What can I do you for?" She swatted a fly that was on the bar with her rag.

"You have food?"

"Yes, we do. Hamburger or cheeseburger, that's all we got. Hamburger is three dollars. Cheeseburger is three twenty-five."

"Then I'll have the cheeseburger. Make it two."

She walked over and grabbed my meal out of the freezer, lit the grill, and in a matter of minutes, the frozen patties started to sizzle.

"So, you own the place?" I asked her.

"Yep. Moved here from Oklahoma City a year ago."

"Really?" I walked over to the door and peeked outside, looking both ways along Route 30. Not a car in sight.

"You get much business?" What I wanted to say was, *Why the hell would anyone move here on purpose?* What sort of business did she need to do to keep this place open?

Assuming her mortgage was around six hundred bucks, then utilities, insurance, another three hundred in electricity to run those big freezers. Cost of goods was let's say 10% of what she retailed for. She'd have to sell about 220 cheeseburgers a month, sans tips. That's just under 8 burgers a day, just to presumably break even.

She was a quarter of the way there with my order. Just might be she was swimming in money. Her closest competition was the Hitchin' Post, nine miles away in Brady. The difference was they had beer and booze—she had flies.

"I came out here with my husband, who worked on the railroad," she said. "He died of a heart attack a few months after we moved here. I bought this place and figured I could fix it up."

Another fly landed on the bar. She swatted at it with the rag.

"Trains honk at you when you're riding?" she asked.

"Yes, frequently. And it scares the shit out of me. But when I look over, the conductor always smiles and waves. So, I smile and a nod back."

The rules regarding horn use for trains were established in the General Code of Operating Rules—"o" was a short blast, "=" was a long blast.

o o o o	To attract the attention of a person or livestock on the track.
= o o o	Instructs flagman to protect the rear of the train
o =	Inspect brake system for leaks

… and so on.

"The railroad," she muttered. "Those bastards…"

And off she went about how bad the railroad and its unions treat their people. Since her husband died, she had been fighting to get his pension, which apparently, they were not willing to give up without a fight.

She handed me my cheeseburgers and continued down her shit list.

"And who are these arrogant liberals who refer to us as fly-over country? What, we don't count because those rich liberals only travel from their million-dollar home in California to their million-dollar condo in New York? They're all assholes!"

I squirted some ketchup on my plate. I wanted to ask her if she had any mayo, but sometimes you had to know when to talk and when to just eat your $3.25 cheeseburger and listen.

Leaving a ten on the counter, I stepped back outside and took a deep breath. The sun felt good. I was full, and North Platte was just fourteen miles away.

North Platte meant nothing to me at first, just another stop on the map. It was the email from my dad sharing how impressed he was that I was all the way to North Platte that made it something.

My dad—I would learn after his passing—was very proud of all four of his kids, not that I doubted that. He was just a bit hands-off with me, as I was always pretty independent. Growing up, I took that to mean he wasn't interested in me. Quite the contrary, he was fascinated and perplexed by all four of his kids. He just gave us a lot of space.

He wrote me a note, which was a very thoughtful, handwritten, seven-page letter, in response to my staying out all night on my sixteenth birthday. I came home in the morning with a neck full of hickeys and the smell of Peach Schnapps on my breath. It was Mother's Day. Mom wasn't impressed.

Hi Cory,

It may seem a little strange getting a letter from your ol' man. But it's through letters that I can express the things that are really in my heart...There's an age old fact that seems to put a strain on every father and son relationship; the fact that every loving father thrives on giving advice to his son and the son rarely—if ever—wants it!

His note continued, where he softly addressed the bad decision I had clearly made. *I don't have to tell you that there's a great deal of peer pressure everywhere you look. We all have it; yes, even us adults...No one gets you into trouble—you get yourself into trouble by letting others decide for you.*

His note finished with:

My faith in your ability to survive in this world a happy person is absolute. Grab at every opportunity and run with it!!!!

You have all my love—Dad

I'd read the letter time and again. It calmed me down when I was anxious. My dad would pass away too soon and too young, but the words in his letter were cherished.

Heading west toward Ogallala, I had only 240 miles to go until Boulder, which was about as close to a midway point as I could figure. I decided that would be three days of riding, although I had not figured out yet where my stops were. When I started this morning, my original goal was Julesburg, Colorado. I had no reason to think that wasn't still possible.

The road was all mine, traffic almost nonexistent. Random train horns continued to jolt me, but I had come to enjoy them. I felt as if I had been accepted in some sort of fraternity of travelers.

I attempted to calculate when the next four toots from a horn would arrive, but never did manage to time them correctly.

My mind wandered. I compared the distance of each mile marker with the distance my cycling computer calculated. Sometimes, they were pretty close. Sometimes, I thought whoever placed the mile marker just didn't give a shit. At other times, I was convinced they were using the metric system.

Somewhere east of Ogallala and west of Gothenburg, I crossed a time zone. It was my first time-zone crossing of the trip.

Growing up in Arizona, we didn't have daylight savings time. It always confused me as a kid. We'd visit grandma in Minnesota in the summer, and it was light until ten, but we had to go to bed at nine. Made no sense.

As a paperboy, I knew the papers had to be delivered before the sun rose over the McDowell Mountains east of Scottsdale. What I didn't grasp was that the sun rose earlier in the summer, thus the papers were late half the year.

"The only reason for time is so that everything doesn't happen at once."

- ALBERT EINSTEIN

It was dry, hot, and mentally exhausting as the elevation began to increase.

Major Stephen Long called this uninhabitable land "the Great American Desert." What he didn't know was the land sat above the Ogallala Aquifer, one of the largest aquifers in the world, holding nearly fourteen trillion gallons of fresh water.

One hundred million years ago, the Western Interior Seaway covered all of Nebraska, along with most of North America. That meant I was biking along an ancient seabed where mosasaurs, plesiosaurs, and ichthyosaurs once swam.

The fossils of these and other prehistoric creatures were scattered throughout the plains. Some gave rise to Native American mythology. The thunderbird and water monster mythos were some examples.

The reptilian water monster, known to the Sioux as the Unhcegila, was a myth possibly created to explain the fossils of the twenty-foot-long mosasaur. The monster ruled everything under the waves and was eventually destroyed by its nemesis the Thunderbird, possibly the fossils of the pterosaur, which, with its forty-foot wingspan, ruled the air.

Ancient people from around the world created myths to understand dinosaur fossils. The myth of the cyclops, it was speculated, might have been born from mammoth skulls, which appeared to have just one eye. The legend of the griffin, with its four legs and beak, was conjured up possibly by the fossil remains of the protoceratops.

I reached Roscoe, Nebraska. Roscoe was a living ghost town housing sixty-four people and offering no businesses, not even a

Subway. I was struck by the names of their seven streets, although I didn't quite understand the logic:

Roscoe 1 Street

Roscoe 2 Street

Roscoe F Street

Roscoe G Street

Roscoe H Street

Roscoe I Street

To mix it up, there was Keystone Roscoe Road, which took you to Keystone just seven miles north, where the Little Church at Keystone sat.

Keystone, in 1908, was a small pioneer town. At the time, the Catholics and Protestants each wanted a church, but the town wasn't big enough to justify two churches. So, they decided to build a church that had a Catholic altar on one end and a Protestant altar at the other. The brilliance was in the design of the pews, which were reversible, allowing churchgoers to face either altar depending on the service. If only all religious conflicts could be resolved so efficiently.

With seven miles to Ogallala, judging from where the sun was sitting in the sky, I felt I could still make Julesburg before the end of the day. That was until I rode up to a sign that was blocking the road.

NO THRU ROAD – LOCAL TRAFFIC ONLY

Beyond the sign, a crater.

Highway 30 was gone. A three-mile-wide hole in the ground laid before me. I could only imagine this was what Dresden looked like after the VIII Bomber Command strafed it in 1945.

It was completely unrideable. While I could only assume to head due west, I couldn't make out where the road would start again. Dismounting my bike, I walked for three miles through this wasteland, sun beating on my face, dust in my eyes. Average speed 2.4 mph and over an hour lost. Well actually, I broke even on the hour as I gained an hour just a few miles back crossing from the Central to Mountain Time Zone.

The pioneers had no road. This was what they dealt with for two thousand miles. With grandma, a crying baby, and a piano in the back of the wagon. The Oregon Trail was an unforgiving mistress who took an estimated thirty thousand lives over forty years.

After seventy-three minutes of walking (I had only my road cycling shoes mind you), the road reappeared. In a few minutes, I was in downtown Ogallala.

I didn't stop. With thirty-two miles to Julesburg, I decided to put my head down and hammer on. I was determined to make Julesburg, but the road had other plans for me.

Two miles past Ogallala, my front tyre went flat. It was as I sat there on the side of the road replacing the tube that I felt the cool winds from the west increase. A front approached. I could smell the rain as dark clouds followed. *Something Wicked This Way Comes*, I thought, to quote Ray Bradbury's famous story title.

Pedaling back to Ogallala, I opted for the Oregon Trail Motel off Highway 30, just past the Petrified Wood Gallery. I wondered how thick that guest book was.

Across the street was a Kwik Trip and Golden Village Chinese restaurant next to that. I picked up a six-pack of beer and an order of beef lo mein, no vegetables, extra spicy, and hunkered down in room number three.

After the fourth beer, I grabbed my camera and snapped a picture of myself in the mirror for the purpose of historic preservation.

History would show when it came to epic journeys, Odysseus had nothing on me.

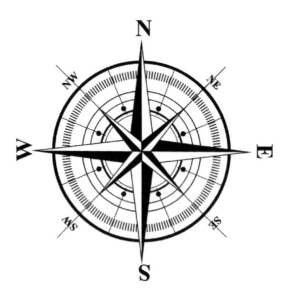

COLORADO

"Colored Red"

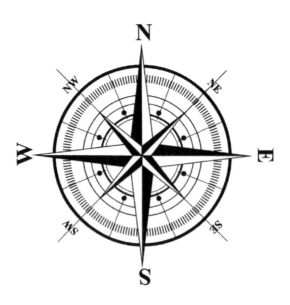

CHAPTER 7

DAY SEVEN

AUGUST 28, 2001

Today's Ride: Ogallala, Nebraska - Sterling, Colorado
Today's Distance: 90 Miles

Though the Oregon Trail Motel didn't offer breakfast, it did have coffee and a stack of foam cups in the front office.

I wasn't that hungry, still pretty bloated from the beer, noodles, and MSG I had for dinner.

Hanging around the motel sipping cups of watered-down coffee, watching as the sun rose over the dusty town, bustling with early morning activity, I waited for the coffee to do its trick before checking out.

When nature called, I preferred a bathroom with an abundant amount of toilet paper over squatting behind a tree. I waited on the curb outside my door.

Perhaps a conversation regarding bowel movements wasn't classy this early in the morning, but real nonetheless. When you found yourself reading a book about someone biking cross-country, you might otherwise ask yourself: *Where did they go to the bathroom whilst out on the open road?*

If the sudden need to shit arose on the road, you could only hope there was a bush, tree, or berm to hide behind. The other option was to keep walking as far away from the road as you could until you were out of sight, or at least blurry. Of course, without the proper equipment (toilet paper), things could get messy. You might find yourself sacrificing a sock. Personally, I had a dresser drawer of mismatched cycling socks at home.

Public options, if you were lucky enough to be in a town or city when things started moving, were:

Restaurants: Now, I would stay clear of anything fancier than a Cracker Barrel. The best were fast food joints, as the bathrooms were typically really clean and out of sight of the counter (so you could get in and out without running into an employee).

Truck Stops: If you came across one of those truck stop fortresses like a BP or Bosselman, take it. Nobody would give you two looks, even if you were dressed in Lycra. The bathrooms were surprisingly clean, and there was typically an abundance of stalls.

Gas Stations: You knew you were in trouble when you asked the attendant for a key and he said the bathroom was outside around back. Check to see if there was any toilet paper in the room before starting. You might find rust stains on the sink and toilets surrounded by a lake of urine. The whole process would become an exercise in squatting. By no means did you want to make any sort of physical contact with anything in that room. Lift the seat with your shoe, flush the toilet with a hand wrapped liberally with a paper towel. It was probably best to find a tree.

So, you could see why I opted to wait before I left Ogallala.

About five miles out of Ogallala, the shoulder disappeared. Traffic was light, and as I conquered a climb a half-mile south of California Hill, a million sunflowers turned the fields yellow.

California Hill was the first major hill the pioneers had to overcome after the Great Plains. It was a 240-foot climb over one mile. They pulled, dragged, and pushed their covered wagons all day to get over this hill. Today, we pressed our foot on the accelerator with just a little more pressure while sipping a latte.

A 240-foot elevation gain over a mile was about a 4.5% grade. What did a 4.5% grade look like? Steep enough to get you out of the saddle and putting a little more effort into every pedal stroke.

SLOPES, GRADES, AND OTHER MATH
I THOUGHT I'D NEVER NEED

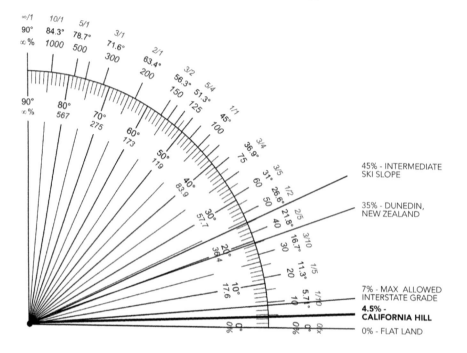

The maximum grade allowed on the Dwight D. Eisenhower National System of Interstate and Defense Highways, also known as the Interstate Highway System, was 7%.

The steepest road in the world was Baldwin Street in Dunedin, New Zealand at 35%. It was created by a bunch of Englishmen who laid out streets in a grid on a map in Britain, no doubt sipping cognac, with absolutely no clue as to the topography of the region.

"His Majesty's dominions, on which the sun never sets," wrote Christopher North. A few miles outside of Ogallala a sign appeared.

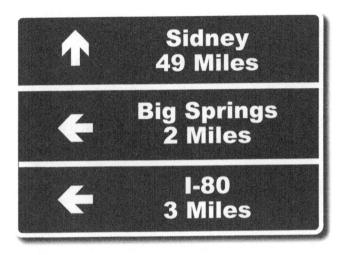

Just past the sign, on the southeast corner of the intersection, was a rundown service station that sat there as a subtle reminder of a time before the interstate. Three pumps and a handful of deserted vehicles littered the lot, spending their final days turning to rust. Everything here was someone else's history.

It was the sort of place I typically would make an effort to break into and explore, to see what treasures might have been inside. Who was going to know? Who would care? There must have been a *No Trespassing* sign, but I couldn't find it.

What if, after breaching the four-by-ten particle board barrier, inside was a top-secret nuclear silo base? It could happen, I mean why was this building still standing out here—alone. Abandoned. Hiding in plain sight.

In 2001, the United States alone had stockpiled over 10,500 warheads. There were silos all over the place. Just west of where I stood, there were fifty-five LGM-30 Minuteman intercontinental ballistic missile silos, managed by the 321st Missile Squadron. Just a phone call and two key twists away from ending it all.

Movies such as *Red Dawn* and *War Games* explored those possibilities during my formative years and fueled our collective imaginations about secret government installations. In an episode of 1986's *Buck Rogers in the 25th Century*, Buck Rogers met the president of the United States in a secret bunker under Mount Rushmore. Truth be told, behind Abraham Lincoln's frontal lobe at Mount Rushmore was a secret room—the Hall of Records. Inside of which was supposedly stored the US Constitution, Declaration of Independence, and Bill of Rights. The thought of a secret network of tunnels under an abandoned gas station wasn't too far of a stretch.

Bidi bidi bidi, what's up Buck?[32]

State Highway 138 lost its importance after I-76 was laid down. Now it was part of thousands of miles of lonely blue highways.[33]

---

32 How Buck Rogers's robot servant Twiki would always greet him.
33 Defined by author William Least Heat-Moon as "small, forgotten, out of the way roads connecting rural America which were drawn in blue on the old-style Rand McNally road atlas."

Cowboy boots topped random posts between Big Springs and the border of Colorado. Cowboys took old, worn-out boots and placed them on posts as tributes to a dead horse or lost friend. It was the sort of gesture that gave the West its mystique and romance. Amidst all the harsh rawness, the heart still cherished those special bonds.

Somewhere between Big Springs and the Colorado border.

It wasn't much in the way of a border crossing. No gas station or discounted cigarettes. Just a sign reading,

WELCOME TO COLORFUL COLORADO.

I leaned my bike against the sign, and took a picture. State number four.

Four states didn't seem like much unless one thought about the size of these particular four states.

Nebraska, for example, was bigger than each of the following countries: Cuba, Ireland, Austria, Portugal, South Korea, North Korea, Greece, Cambodia, Syria, Senegal, and Kyrgyzstan.

In fact, you could put the following five countries together within the borders of Nebraska: Belgium, the Netherlands, Luxembourg, Slovenia, and Switzerland.

There was a saying: "In the United States, one hundred years is old, and in Europe, one hundred miles is far."

Colorado conjured up majestic mountains, gorgeous gorges, waterfalls, bald eagles, fresh air, elk, bighorn sheep, adventure, snow skiing powder, Grizzly Adams, and John Denver's "Rocky Mountain High." What was forgotten was that 40% of Colorado was part of the Great Plains. Only a line on a map separated the Nebraska plains from Colorado's plains. From where I stood, Colorado was flat, quiet, lonely, unattractive, and not at all colorful.

I was still 150 miles away from getting a glimpse of the Rocky Mountains, but I could see the grain elevator in Julesburg, which was a welcome sight. Another checkpoint reached.

The town of Julesburg was practically vacant. My tyres made a crunching sound as I rolled into town. I stopped at a little diner off Cedar Street. The scene felt eerie as if some nefarious presence was hiding behind curtained windows. Perhaps I'd be approached by an overly friendly sheriff who, with a forced smile, would encourage me to just move along. Inform me the town doesn't take kindly to strangers. The next few days would evolve into a cat-and-mouse game between me and the locals. Two children would quickly gain my trust. They'd show me various secret passageways and, ultimately, an ancient text spelling out the curse of the town. It would not end well. The townspeople would win, catching me only after I was betrayed by the two children, who would lead me down a staircase and into a prepared sacrificial lair, surrounded by fifty-eight hooded locals all chanting in an ancient language. I'd be strapped to a stone altar. The knife would fall quickly, and the beast would be appeased… until the next victim stumbled into town.

D&J Café offered an all-you-can-eat lunch for $5.75. I had two plates of spaghetti and a big bowl of fruit salad.

Aside from the waitress, there were three blue-hairs[34] at a four top. They stared at me as if I had stolen their cat.

What if they were part of a satanic cult, and my sacrifice would give them back their youth? The blue-hairs appeared innocent, but Minnie Castevet[35] was innocent-looking as well.

They'd have to catch me first! They didn't look like speed was on their side, but they might have supernatural strength. They might be 1,400-year-old vampires. I smiled at them. One of them replied with a scoff.

Before Julesburg was founded, the town that stood here was referred to as "The Wickedest City in the West." Just the sort of place a notorious stagecoach bandit by the name of Jules Beni could thrive.

Beni, up to no good, was finally arrested by a fella by the name of Jake Slade. Neither a fan of the other. Slade would eventually gun down Beni in 1861. Slade, being either batshit crazy, which may be confirmed by an acquaintance that said the name Jack Slade "became synonymous for all that is infamous and cruel in human character;" or Slade simply hating Beni so intensely, he took Beni's dead body, tied it to a post, shot off his fingers, and cut off his ears.

One ear he used as a watch fob, and the other he sold for booze.

To put a period on how insane the Wild West was, the locals, due to some sort of bizarre admiration for Jules Beni, honored him

---

34 An elderly woman with white or gray hair that has been tinted blue
35 Neighbor and member of the local witch's coven in *Rosemary's Baby*

by naming their city Julesburg. So, it wasn't a far stretch to think evil founded the town of Julesburg.

Sterling was fifty-eight miles away, and the clouds had all passed. The skies were clear as far as you could see. It was hot with no wind.

Oh, wait, you wanted to know what happened to Jack Slade? In 1864, he got drunk and ornery one night in Virginia City, Montana, where apparently the punishment for such antics was a good ol' fashioned lynching. Age thirty-three. A scrap of paper was attached near Slade that read "3-7-77." It was assumed those where the dimensions of his grave: three feet wide, seven feet long, and seventy-seven inches deep.

Had that been the punishment in Winona, Minnesota, in 1989, yours truly would have also been strung up. Age nineteen.

After my meal, I found my back tyre was flat. I sulked a bit. Maybe it was one of the blue-hairs trying to trap me here. I looked at them through the window. They stared back out of the corners of their cataract-y eyes.

I went through the flat tyre procedure, every once in a while making sure the blue-hairs weren't making a move on me. Tyre repaired and bike reassembled, I coasted toward Sterling. Over two blocks, my front tyre deflated. Along with my soul in this soulless town.

I checked behind me. No blue-hairs, no sheriff, no children. Just me and my bike. I needed to get out of this town. In all its silence, I swear I could hear someone sharpening an athamé.[36]

Without having to remove my pack, I could fix the front tyre. It was a quick change. I ran my fingers along the inside of the tyre to check for a nail or piece of glass. I found a small thorn—how Gothic—which I removed.

About a half-mile out of town, the rear tyre went flat again. There was some bad juju going on here. I checked the tube—two punctures. I used my patch kit, leaving me with just three more patches.

Continuing on another mile, both tyres went flat.

"WHAT THE FUCK?" I yelled to the heavens.

It was ninety-eight degrees, and there was no shade. Out of anger, I threw my pack fifteen feet into a field. Then, I flipped the bike upside down and removed both wheels.

As I sunk into a seat on the dirt shoulder, I felt a few thorns puncture my ass. I jumped up. Sand burs. There were sand burs everywhere!

Better than Sand People, with their gaffe sticks and banthas,[37] I thought, but I wasn't sure.

Clearing the ground around me, I returned to replacing my tubes when a Colorado state trooper pulled up.

---

36 Ceremonial blade used in black magic arts.
37 Reference to *Star Wars* when Luke Skywalker came across Sand People and was saved by Obi-Wan Kenobi

He rolled down his window, looked at all my shit scattered about, my wheel-less bike, and me sitting in the dirt. In one breath, he said the following: "How you doing everything okay have a good ride!"

And then he took off. Didn't even stop.

"Dick," I mumbled, flipping him off when he was well out of sight. I mean, they still might lynch people in these parts. I should just be happy he wasn't an overly friendly sheriff from Julesburg.

Eighteen minutes later, I was riding again. I had one tube left and two patches. I thought about the Dalai Lama and the pointlessness of worrying about my situation.

"If you have fear of some pain or suffering, you should examine whether there is anything you can do about it. If you can, there is no need to worry about it; if you cannot do anything, then there is also no need to worry."

Although when the Dalai Lama said that, he wasn't two punctures away from being stranded in northeastern Colorado, only a few miles outside of a town that definitely sacrificed strangers.

Just past the Julesburg airport, my front tyre went flat. I had no patience to repair another flat. I started walking, for no other reason than to think about my options and keep forward progress.

Did the pioneers stop when they came across hardships? Probably. I mean, what did you do when a wooden wagon wheel crumbled one hundred miles from nowhere?

Most likely, they died shortly after, from exposure, starvation, or self-inflicted gunshot wound. Or maybe they built a house and started a business fixing wagon wheels for other pioneers. Why else would people live out here? Somebody's wagon went to shit, and that was that. Welcome home, kids!

That was where the money was. Screw digging for gold in California, sell off your shovels and picks at inflated prices.

If you'd ever owned one, the sound of the Volkswagen air-cooled boxer engine was easily recognizable. The lifters gave it away.

Walking with my head down, kicking the dirt, feeling sorry for myself, I heard the sound of an air-cooled Volkswagen approaching.

A dude in a 1968 VW Bus that was in need of some restoration stopped next to me. "Hey, man. You got everything you need?"

"I'm down to my last tube and patches."

"Ha ha. Yeah man, those sand burs will wreak havoc."

I nodded in agreement. I was not in a pleasant mood and really didn't want to talk.

"You know, there is a bike shop in Julesburg."

"You're shitting me!"

"Get in. I'll take you. I'm heading that way"

By the diner with the blue-hairs, I got out of the bus.

"It's just down Pine Street," the driver said, pointing. "Good luck, man."

Maybe the blue-hairs really were part of a satanic cult, and Julesburg was—perhaps still—the wickedest city on the Plains. I couldn't seem to leave. The town was Ravenhurst,[38] and I was Pete Danner, cursed to return no matter which road I traveled down.

---

38 The estate in the movie *The Legacy* from where Pete Danner tries to escape, but no
   matter what road he travels, they all lead back to Ravenhurst.

Down Pine Street, there it was, Tri-N-Bike Sports.

A handwritten note was taped to the door: *Closed until Aug 29.*

"Tomorrow? They don't open until tomorrow. Great, just frick-ing great!"

I looked around. Still no people. No cars, no church bells, no trains. I fixed my front flat and decided that I was just going to ride right down the middle of US-138. I hadn't seen a car since half-past whenever, and there had to be far fewer sand burs in the middle of the road.

Traffic can yield to me. I am the king of the all I can see! So says the one-eyed cyclist.[39]

Jim Morrison was the Lizard King. He chose the lizard as his shamanistic alter ego. A creature that sheds its skin perhaps gave Jim the feeling of constant renewal. I would imagine every morning that Morrison woke up in an un-altered state gave him a sense of renewal.

Who was I kidding? I was no Jim Morrison. I was no king.

Caption Kirk had Tribbles; I had sandburs.

Seven miles later, I arrived in Ovid with no flats. That was until I got to Main Street, where my front tyre deflated.

I wanted to throw my bike into the lake, but there was no lake—there wasn't even a retention pond. There was no traffic, no people, not even a stray dog. It was as if I was injected into the town of Oakwood in the *Twilight Zone* episode "Where Is Everybody?"

---

39 In reference to the philosopher Desiderius Erasmus Roterodamus's quote, "in the land of the blind, the one-eyed man is king."

So, where *was* everybody!?

Two patches, fifty miles ahead of me, 103 degrees, and a defeated attitude. The only thing that could cheer me up was an ice-cold Coca-Cola.

Yes, a Coke and a smile. I could teach the world to sing, *in perfect harmony*, if I had me a Coke.

Lucky for me, a Coke machine was just a half-block down. Digging through my pack, I found fifty cents. I walked down the sidewalk, singing that famous 1971 Coca-Cola song.

"And furnish it with love…Grow apple trees and honey bees… And snow white turtle doves…"

I dropped the two shiny coins into the machine and continued singing: "I'd like to buy the world a Coke…"

I heard the mechanism grind and the can drop. But, the can just didn't drop all the way.

"Oh, come on! Are kidding me?"

I hit the machine, tried rocking it—those things were heavy. The can made no progress.

I kicked the machine a few times, then took a deep breath. Then, I leaned my head against the front of the machine in defeat.

I turned and scanned the town. Every building seemed vacant. I was convinced I would be stranded, until I saw it. Down the street, another block east, the front wheel of a bicycle stuck out of an alcove.

Was that a bike wheel? Maybe I could salvage the tube and tyre, take a spoke or two. Shit, just take the whole wheel. I could strap it on the back of my bike somehow. I'd make it work.

I approached the wheel. The wheel turned into a bike, then a second bike. Holding these two bikes were the first cyclists I had seen on the entire trip—a man and a woman eating bananas.

"Hey, guys," I said, as cheerily as I could muster. I had to rethink my plan of taking the whole wheel.

"Hi."

"Hey."

They didn't have much personality. Could have been members of the blue-hair cult, so I kept my guard up.

"How you doing?" I asked.

"Fine," one of them offered. For a second, I thought that would be it. "Are you biking far?"

"Well, today I'm shooting for Sterling. Started in Minneapolis a few days ago."

"We left Sterling this morning. We are heading to Julesburg. We own the bike shop there."

I knew it! They probably had matching sacrificial robes and were once again directing me to what was becoming the inescapable town of Julesburg.

"No way!" I said, trying to play it cool. "I was just there, wanted to buy some tubes. I'm down to just two patches."

"Sand burs," said the woman. "They'll getcha."

"Did you just do an out and back to Sterling?"

"Sort of," said the man. "I'm a dentist and work every other week at the prison down there. We prefer to ride our bikes, since it's just a day's ride."

Dentist! Of course, the perfect profession for one versed in the dark arts.

"Look," said the satanic dentist. "We have some extra tubes. Take these."

He handed me nine tubes.

"Oh man," I said. "I just tried to buy a Coke with my last fifty cents. I don't have any cash on me."

"Just enjoy your ride," the woman said as they finished their bananas and hopped back on their bikes.

They were most certainly the nicest satanists I had ever met.

I fixed my flat and made it to Sedgwick with a newfound sense of invincibility. I mean, nine tubes! That was like having a million dollars. I was unstoppable.

When I arrived in Sedgwick, I was totally out of water. There were no service stations in sight, nor were there any people. Maybe a few blocks off US-138, I could have found a gas station or bodega, but I didn't bother exploring.

Crook was seventeen miles further, and upon arriving, I stopped at the Tumble Weed Cafe & Bar. I ordered a beer first, gone by the time I ordered my meal—a beef steak with a slice of French Silk Pie and another beer. Because every once in a while, you had to treat yourself. Especially after escaping the clutches of Julesburg and having become an expert in the fine art of fixing flat tyres.

I followed up my meal with a pint of water and asked the server if they could fill up my water bottles.

The Tumble Weed did not take credit cards, as they didn't have any sort of internet connection. Nope, they were cash or check only.

I had exactly zero dollars on me, but I did have my checkbook. They were certainly a trusting bunch, willing to accept a personal, out-of-state check for an eighteen-dollar meal, from a scrubby-looking cyclist headed westbound from nowhere.

Two blocks south of the Tumble Weed, a house had a sign on the front door that read: *Please close gate. Don't step on snakes.*

I looked around for snakes and pedaled as quickly as I could away from the house.

As far as I was concerned, every snake could kill you. I knew that wasn't true, but my Malebolge[40] would involve serpents, that was for sure.

---

40 The eighth circle of Hell in Dante's *Inferno*.

The ride from Crook to Sterling was without incident. I mean, there were no flat tyres, no mechanicals, no dogs, no snakes, no wind, no hills… nothing. I couldn't have been happier.

Known as the Queen City of the Plains, Sterling, Colorado, felt like a metropolis compared to the past few towns I'd passed through. It had everything—bars, restaurants, a library, grocery stores, even a few homeless people. On the south side of town, I came across The Crest Motel.

It was a quaint place that looked like someone added a row of rooms off the back of the family home.

Wiped out, I filled out the registration card, paid my seventy-six dollars, and asked where the nearest grocery store was.

"Just a stone's throw away," said the clerk. "Around the corner, two blocks."

I rode over, pulled my bike into the store, and leaned it next to the ATM. I didn't feel the need to bother digging out the lock.

A bag boy gave me an affirmative nod. "Nice bike."

Twenty-one glorious rows of everything. I didn't bother asking if my room had a microwave. I assumed it didn't, so that cut out the entire frozen food section. I didn't have a can opener, so no tuna or beans. I focused my attention on the deli counter. Usually, offerings included burritos, fried chicken, and mac and cheese, one of the greatest food inventions known to man. Thank you, Thomas Jefferson.

The hot counter was closed. However, in the cooler sat what appeared to be my next great idea. Eight precut slices each of ham, roast beef, and turkey, separated by eight precut slices each of cheddar, pepper jack, and Swiss cheese. Meat and cheese—my two most important food groups—for a mere $8.95. Plus, it was easy, requiring no utensils or heating.

I purchased the deli tray and returned to my room. The dread didn't hit me right away. In fact, it wasn't until I was naked, preparing to enter the shower, when I realized I didn't have any beer. That's when I knew I had perhaps made a rash decision at the grocery store, too blinded by my deli tray to get the necessities. A shower without beer? Why bother?

Now, I'd made plenty of bad decisions in my life, and this deli plate was one of them. What the hell was I thinking? A deli plate? What attracted me to this round, plastic container of days-old cold cuts and sweating cheese? Forget the beer, I didn't even have the sense to get crackers!

I sat on the bed, disgusted with myself. I was at a grocery store. I could have picked up chips and salsa, beef jerky, a box of Cheez-Its, beer.

I turned on the television for some company. CNN was showing a special—thirty-eight years ago on this day, Dr. Martin Luther King, Jr. gave his famous "I Have A Dream" Speech on the steps of the Lincoln Memorial in Washington, DC. A defining moment for the civil rights movement in America.

The powerful stench of roast beef slapped me across the face when I opened the cover of the deli tray. I pushed the entire tray aside, pulled off the comforter, and laid down, deciding it was better to just go to bed. I, too, had a dream. I dreamt I hadn't purchased this deli plate. It was a sand burr in my side.

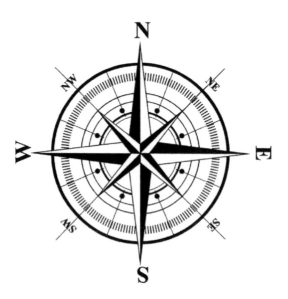

CHAPTER 8

DAY EIGHT

AUGUST 29, 2001

Today's Ride: Sterling, Colorado - Boulder, Colorado
Today's Distance: 121 Miles

Lying in bed, I stared at the ceiling, processing the day before. I tried to separate what really happened from what I imagined. A small town of satanists, searching for their next sacrificial lamb. Perhaps they followed me to Sterling? Were they waiting in a white van, like those CIA agents back in Minnesota?

Not real.

I thought about the house with the snakes—very much real. According to my Uncle Johnny, the self-assigned family historian: throughout September 1941, Milbert (my grandpa), an officer in the Army, was bivouacking[41] in the swamplands of Louisiana, sleeping in a pup tent that consisted of a roof and sides, no floor.

One night, while out in the field, a Texas coral snake got into his sleeping bag and bit him. While highly toxic, the bite was rarely fatal because the fangs were small and only injected small amounts of

---

41 A military encampment made with tents or improvised shelters, usually without shelter or protection from enemy fire.

venom. Still, the bite was bad enough that Milbert was hospitalized for an extended period of time.

It was because of the Louisiana Maneuvers—which, in 1941, involved four hundred thousand US Army troops participating in war games to prepare them to enter the war in Europe—that Milbert refused to go camping. He could never fathom why people would purposely seek out the discomforts of sleeping anywhere but a nice warm bed.

I could not imagine waking up with a snake in my bed. I would lose my shit. Finding one in my sleeping bag while I was in it? Absolutely not.

Waking up to a room-temperature deli plate was a close second. I failed to seal the cover tightly before going to bed—the smell of roast beef and ham weighed heavy in the room.

My immediate goal was to pack up, get dressed, and get the hell out of this room as quickly as possible. I took one last look at the deli plate before shutting the door, leaving it for the rats.

I smiled as I imagined its final scream—"Do it to Julia!"[42]

Cory - 0

Deli Plate - 1

How was it that hotels weren't riddled with mice and rats? The rooms I had stayed in on this trip had surely been littered with pizza boxes and other food scraps over the years. And yet, no critters.

---

42 In George Orwell's *1984*, Winston has a cage with two hungry rats strapped to his face. He must choose between betraying his lover Julia or have the rats released to eat him alive. He opts to betray Julia.

Hostels in Central America were not the same experience. I once woke up in El Salvador with a cow poking its head through the window of my *habitación*.

I left one crumb of bread on my counter at home, and suddenly a family of mice had parked their mouse-sized Airstream in my kitchen and invited the in-laws over. It was a wonderment.

Game plan:

- ☑ Scan the street for a white van

- ☑ Breakfast in Brush

- ☑ Call Freddy (my cousin) from Fort Lupton

- ☑ Have Freddy pick me up somewhere between Fort Lupton and Boulder

- ☑ Dinner in Boulder

The owner of the motel told me last night it was 117 miles to Denver. The map said 126. The mileage sign said 138. I swore to God, I was going to make it my life's work to address these grievous mileage inconsistencies.

Brush was just thirty-five miles away. I wanted to put a few miles between me and the land of sand burs, blue-haired occultists, and deli plates before I stopped for a meal.

I passed through the towns of Atwood, Merino, Beta, Hillrose, and Camden, and crossed the South Platte River. I made it to Brush—or *Brush!*, as the sign said, emphasizing the town's "can-do attitude."

Coasting down Edison Street, I passed True Grits Steakhouse and Willow Coffee. Neither drew me in. I was feeling really good and decided to take the energy and momentum I had and make a charge for Fort Morgan, just ten miles west. I'd stop for breakfast there.

Since Sterling, I had been riding along US Route 6. Just before Brush, it connected with US Route 34. It was hard to tell from looking at the map of Colorado if there was a frontage road along I-76, and I didn't want to make an assumption. No more chances… not today anyway.

In Fort Morgan, I had breakfast at Zazzy Café and then stopped at the library to access the internet.

It was the end of the month, and my mortgage was due. I was renting my house out to some college girls. What an incredible world, when after biking for a week plus, I could get on a computer in an unfamiliar town and pay my mortgage and utilities. Of course, now, in the world of smart phones, that might seem quaint. But in 2001, it was remarkable.

An over-excited librarian told me the safest route to Fort Lupton would be to head south on County Road 1805, then west on County Road Q. This route would also take me past her daughter's house.

"Wave as you pass by," the librarian instructed.

Once at Q, I took a right heading due west for fourteen miles to County Road 52. The intersection of Q and CR-52 was about a mile east of Wiggins. In retrospect, I should have gone to Wiggins and filled my water bottles. But I didn't. Instead, I turned south.

There was nothing in the way of a town along County Road 52 from Wiggins until Hudson, CO, which was forty-one miles from where I was. So sayeth the map.

It was a remarkably hot day with no wind at all. The air was dry. It felt like I was cycling in an oven. To make things worse, eight miles south of Wiggins, I ran out of water.

Thirty-two miles until the next town. Random dust devils kicked up dust on an otherwise stagnant day. My throat was sore. I rubbed my tongue across my teeth to generate some saliva. What little saliva I could produce became thick mud from the dust. I attempted to spit it out but failed.

A few more miles and my head was pounding. I had heatstroke. I was dizzy and weak, but I had to keep going. I had no choice. I hadn't seen a car or truck in thirty minutes.

A branch lay across the shoulder up ahead, but there were no trees. Just open farmland. Open farmland, this road, and a branch. A branch that upon approaching was in fact a four-foot rattlesnake, sunbathing on the asphalt. I swerved at the last minute to avoid the serpent, my heart rate spiked, adrenalin pumping.

Shit! I thought. *Assume all branches are snakes until proven otherwise.*

I stopped and looked back. The rattlesnake had coiled itself up, equally surprised.

"What was that?" the rattlesnake was probably saying to itself. "I was up all night chasing field mice. Can't a rattlesnake get a nap in without being bothered?"

The sun-tanning serpent sent my already vulnerable body into DEFCON 2. Additionally, I started to get chills, one of the many signs of heat exhaustion. Other symptoms I experienced included: muscle cramps, dizziness, and a headache.

The road ahead was a melting mirage. I accepted this stretch of road as my final resting spot.

"DAMN!"

I almost didn't see it—another rattlesnake! I just missed it. My nerves were shot. I could barely swallow. Dizzy, I smacked my lips and breathed through my nose. My tongue was swollen. I pressed on in hopes of a random gas station or convenience store.

Twelve miles after running out of water, I came across an oasis in the desert.

I could see no earthly reason for this church to exist where it was, but the Kiowa Creek Community Church sat there right off County Road 52.

Outside was a group of women having a picnic, also for no earthly reason.

"Howdy," I said, walking toward them with my bike. I struggled to speak.

"Well, hello," they said.

"Say, y'all wouldn't happen to have some water?" It was all I could do to get the words out.

"Why yes, we do. The church is open. Go right on inside and you help yourself to whatever you need."

I went in, filled up my water bottles, soaked my head under the spigot, and drank until I couldn't drink anymore.

Not being in any sort of rush, I sat inside until my head stopped pounding and studied my map. Every muscle in my body was twitching, the slightest movement caused my muscles to instantly knot up. I needed more time to rest and recover. It was still twenty-five miles to Hudson.

The left side of my body was burnt from the southerly sun. Water blisters were forming on my exposed skin. I drank more water and rested until my muscles stopped twitching. I was there for an hour, maybe an hour and a half, before I decided to hammer out the twenty-five miles needed to get closer to wrapping up this day.

"Thank you very much, ladies," I said as I stepped back outside.

"Where are you coming from?"

"Started in Minneapolis about a week ago. Hey, how much further is it to Hudson?"

"Oh, just twenty minutes or so."

I looked at my bike and looked at them. Clearly, their frame of reference was car travel.

I walked back toward the road, climbed onto the bike, and set off. As I arrived in Hudson, I could start to make out the Rocky Mountains in the distance. Seeing them brought forth a feeling of overwhelming accomplishment. I wasn't there yet, but I felt like I had made it.

At a gas station, I bought myself a Snickers and a Coca-Cola, then called my cousin Freddy.

"This is Fredrick."

"Hey, Freddy! Cory here. What are you doing?"

"Cory! Where are you?"

"I'm in Hudson."

"Where is Hudson? Are you on your cycle? I didn't know it took so long to ride a motorcycle cross-country. Can't they go more than a hundred miles a day?"

"Dude, I'm on a bicycle. I pedaled out here."

"What?"

"Look, I'm on County Road 52, about forty miles east of Boulder. Can you come pick me up?"

"Sure thing. I can't leave for another hour, though, but I'll head out when I can."

"See you in a few hours. You can't miss me. I'm the scrubby guy on a bike."

I left Hudson pretty excited. I planned on staying in Boulder for about a week. Wasn't sure what I was going to do when I got there, but I knew I wouldn't be riding my bike. At least for a few days.

After an hour of biking, I came upon some road construction. The flag guy stopped me.

"How's it going?" he asked.

"Just fine," I said. "Do you know how many miles it is to Boulder?"

"Dude, I don't even know where Boulder is." He paused. "I'm from Kansas. Which way is Boulder anyway?"

"Kansas is east. Boulder is west," I said. The flag guy looked confused. "The sun rises in the east and sets in the west, that's how you can tell which way's which."

I didn't think he understood what I was telling him. He was probably stoned. I knew I'd be stoned if I had to hold a sign all day in the middle of nowhere.

Traffic was backed up behind me, and I was about to enter a half-mile stretch of road with no shoulder.

"Hey man," said the flag guy, "you go ahead now. I'll hold the cars back a couple of minutes so you can get clear of the construction."

"Thanks!"

I saluted him and took off.

Just after passing I-25, I heard a car honking frantically. It was Freddy. My odometer read 944 miles. I had crossed the Rubicon.

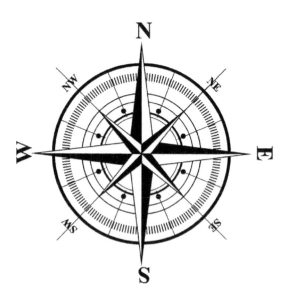

BOULDER, COLORADO

Intermission

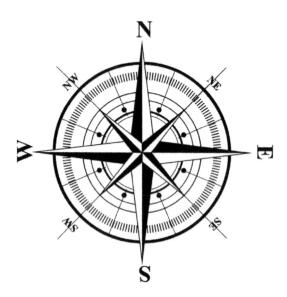

CHAPTER 9

INTERMISSION

AUGUST 29, 2001 - SEPTEMBER 9, 2001

Freddy rented out the basement of a house in Boulder near the Flatirons. The town of Boulder was the perfect place to take time to reflect on the trip. I gathered a few much-needed supplies, such as a clean shirt, a second pair of shorts, and a sweater.

I collected the package I had sent from Redwood Falls on Day 1, enjoyed overpriced chai, and got caught up on my journal.

I slept on a futon in the living room next to his dog Frey.[43]

To stay busy during the day, I spent a few hours helping Freddy with his new venture, Dagoba. Dagoba was an organic chocolate company that was in its infancy at the time of my visit. Freddy worked

43 In Norse mythology, Frey is sacral kingship, battle, virility, peace, and prosperity, with sunshine and fair weather, and with a good harvest.

the various flavors like an alchemist, hand-pouring each bar. After they cooled, I weighed them to assure they were exactly two and a half ounces, then wrapped each one by hand. Looking back, had I invested ten thousand dollars into his company then, I'd be writing this book from my sailboat in the San Blas Islands.

Freddy making chocolate.

I might as well tell you how I was funding this trip. Back in 1996, my lease was up, and I decided to buy a house. I picked my real estate agent solely off his phone number, 333-JOHN. He had advertised his services in City Pages, a local Minneapolis rag with a lot of opinions, concert listings, preferred restaurants, and two back pages full of sex advertisements.

333-JOHN liked to get stoned and drive around looking at houses.

My dad wasn't convinced buying a house was a good idea, but he loaned me the $3,100 down payment on the $62,000 three-bedroom, one-bath house. In six months, I had him paid back with interest.

With the help of some friends, I gutted the 1909 former farmhouse down to the studs, then reinsulated, rewired, replumbed, and refinished the entire thing.

My neighbor, Rocky, told me that at one point, a guy that went by the name "Little Tony" used to own the house. Little Tony apparently ran numbers for the mob (confirmed by the fourteen phone lines he had wired in the house). Rocky told me that Little Tony had a habit of stashing money in the walls. This information sped up the demolition process considerably. Unfortunately, the only thing I found in the walls was air and eighty-seven-year-old trash left behind by the original construction crew.

My next-door neighbor told me she was planning on selling, so I decided to stretch myself as financially thin as possible in hopes my gamble would pay off, and tried to buy her house. It was massive— five bedrooms, three baths, two fireplaces, grand staircase, double lot up on a hill overlooking a park with a view of the Minneapolis skyline in the distance, and two two-car garages.

She also had fifteen cats that pissed everywhere inside the house, thousands of moldy books, smoked, and no sense of smell. The smell of her house was so powerful that if she opened her windows, I had to shut mine. When she listed it for sale, one could barely walk into the house. Realtors sat outside when holding open houses. It was a fierce, powerful smell, but I wanted the house. I saw the potential.

Before making an offer, I spent some time learning all the plants she had around the yard to earn some favorable points. As we strolled through the yard one day, I pointed and said, "Oh my, I just love these hostas. Is that lamb's ear? Just lovely."

Then, my over-thinking interfered with what was a successful points-gathering mission. We stood on the back deck and, glancing at a vine producing flowers, I said, "And I see you have chlamydia."

She stared at me in shock.

"Clematis! I mean clematis! I see you have clematis."

She accepted my apology and my low-ball offer. I fixed the place up and, after hearing of my plant conversation, a friend gave me a brochure that read: "Chlamydia is not a flower."

I sold the first house, pocketed the profits, and rented four of the bedrooms of my newly acquired estate before leaving on this trip. The rent gave me enough cash to cover my mortgage and have some extra.

Although I had plenty of time to think about and plan out the second half of this trip, I spent no time on the matter. Instead, I sat in Boulder, sipping my chai, writing in my journal, staring at the Rocky Mountains—the name, taken from the Cree *as-sin-wata*, which meant, *When seen from across the prairies, they looked like a rocky mass*. It still hadn't sunk in what an epic amount of work it was going to be to get over and across them.

It would be 6,713 feet of climbing—a distance of fifty-two miles to the top and another forty-eight to get to the other side. Over the nearly thousand miles that I had already biked, I had increased in elevation by only 4,500 feet.

I had no real understanding of what the climb would look or feel like. I'd driven over the Rockies countless times, but that was something else entirely. At elevation, even my 1980 R65 BMW motorcycle would struggle to get up and through the Eisenhower-Edwin C. Johnson Memorial Tunnel, mostly because it was carbureted, and the air was so thin.

My stay in Boulder could be summed up in two words: nothing exciting. And that was just fine. Making it to Boulder was an achievement in and of itself. I had never done anything like this before. My only training had been sipping glasses of Jameson, feeling sorry for myself over a breakup with a woman who was, at the time, the love of my life.

I only had myself to blame for the breakup. I was selfish, took her for granted, and was a bit scared of the next step. *Marriage.* We were cohabitating, the cogs and gears of the relationship grinding away—why walk down an aisle? To echo the sentiment of all those commitment phobes who had come before me and would come after me, what was a piece of paper going to prove? I had been in relationships longer than some people's marriages.

We were together for about two years. I never even considered asking her if she wanted to get married. I drifted from her, working longer hours, sleeping with my back to her, filling my time with projects, and dedicating little to our relationship. And then one day, she was gone.

However, the creation myth not only spawned women and men; but with Adam's other rib, it also created the rebound girlfriend (or boyfriend).

The rebound girlfriend and I worked together in the same office, but how it all happened was still a mystery. I didn't recall her being part of my circle of friends, though she went to school with some peers. Perhaps it was a happy hour that turned into a crush that turned into a whirlwind affair. Whatever it was, I was three weeks into it when I found myself heading west to California to meet her at her sister's wedding in Truckee. When I left, I thought of her as my girlfriend, considered us to be in a relationship, but over the first nine days of the trip, I had spent no time thinking about her. I took inventory of my situation. I was in Boulder with just as many miles ahead of me as I had behind me, and I still had plenty of time left of my leave of absence clock.

The last day in Boulder, Freddy's girlfriend Indigo commented while I repacked my gear, "Where's your CamelBak? You'll never make it across the desert with just two water bottles."

"I'm good," I said, annoyed that she would question a seasoned pro such as myself. "I've made it this far with just the two." (Thanks to one miraculous run-in with some church ladies.)

"It's the desert," she continued. "There is nothing out there! You need a CamelBak."

Next thing I knew, I was in her car heading to the local outdoor gear shop.

A CamelBak was a small day pack with a water bladder. I opted for the 4-liter bladder and reluctantly spent seventy dollars to appease my stubborn acquaintance. After our side trip, I finished packing and pumped up my tyres to prepare for a morning departure.

The plan was for a few of us to get together for dinner and drinks that night. Freddy and I managed to get a quick hike in with Frey in the Flatirons before heading downtown. Over too much tequila, we discussed the future and mused about product ideas and ways to implement them. We talked about our lives and how good we'd had it, relatively speaking.

I savored the night. The next morning, I would be alone again, heading west.

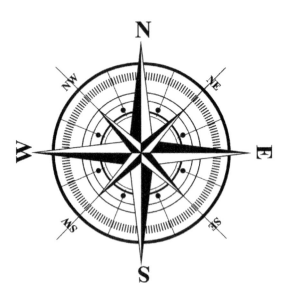

STILL IN COLORADO

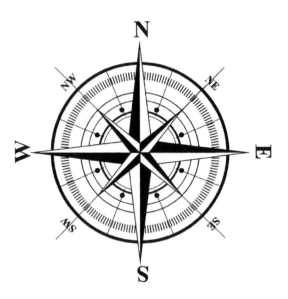

CHAPTER 10

DAY TWENTY

SEPTEMBER 10, 2001

Today's Ride: Boulder, Colorado - Estes Park, Colorado
Today's Distance: 38 Miles

Tequila…I drank too much tequila.

I didn't much like tequila. Unless it was all there was, tequila would be near the bottom of my list when it came to alcohol, perhaps just above Chartreuse.

Even with its fascinating history, Chartreuse was a tough liquid to keep down. Known as *the elixir of long life*, the liquor's recipe was written in an ancient alchemical manuscript. I was seventeen when I first tried it. My buddy Mark and I put a solid dent in a bottle of it on our first go. That drinking session alone should have added a couple of decades to our lives.

I had met Mark in my junior year of high school after my family relocated to Hastings, Minnesota. We became fast friends and spent long weekends in his parents' basement. Mark was a musical savant. He could pick up an instrument and have it figured out in a day. I spent countless weekends with Mark, him creating music and me writing lyrics, both of us taking nips out of his dad's whiskey bottle and occasionally sneaking out to a party in search of women. We drifted apart after our freshman year of university and completely lost touch a couple of years after that.

Meanwhile, I woke up in Boulder, hungover. There wasn't enough water to quench my thirst.

I reviewed my day's plan, which was pretty simple: Get to Granby.

My first stop, just thirty-eight miles north-by-northwest of Boulder, was Estes Park—piece of cake. I could do thirty-eight miles *lickity split.*

Once there, I'd have a late breakfast, ride over the Rocky Mountains and coast into Granby, just ninety-eight miles from Boulder. No problemo. I'd done ninety-eight miles in one day. It was just that I wasn't at altitude.

With bike in tow, I dragged myself up the stairs from the basement apartment and started pedaling north down Broadway. My head was pounding, my mouth dry as the Atacama.[44] I could only see clearly out of one eye. My equilibrium was nonexistent.

This is a bad idea, I thought, *maybe I should spend one more night in Boulder?*

Everything around me was spinning. I could barely muster the strength to get to twelve miles per hour, then had to stop after three miles to rest my head on the handlebars. I spit, aiming for the ground before the wind blew, and it landed on my shoe. I shook my head and drank a full bottle of water.

44 The Atacama Desert is one of the driest places in the world.

Tequila - 1
Cory - 0

Ninety-eight endless minutes, seventeen torturous miles, and 850 miserable feet of elevation gain later, I reached Lyons.

Elevation at Lyons was 5,400 feet. The sun, closer now, was beating down on me. The temperature was near eighty. I desperately wanted to throw up, crawl into my sleeping bag at Johnson Park, and sleep the rest of the day. Maybe also chug a few Gatorades and grab some Chinese food.

I accepted that there was no way I was going to make Granby. I might not even make Estes Park, and that was just twenty-one miles from Lyons. Estes Park was an additional three thousand feet of elevation gain, a fact that wasn't fully clear to me when I headed out of Lyons after skipping my planned late breakfast.

The road to Estes Park was hell at 3.6 miles per hour. I swear the road stretched ahead of me at a forty-five-degree angle. I ticked off each mile, a slow procession at the speed I was going.

Using *speed* to describe my pace was an insult to the word.

I had nine marathons under my belt, and I could say for certain that my marathon pace was faster than the pace I was currently cranking out on my bike. There was beauty all around me, and all I could do was drool onto my top tube, swear, and try to keep from swerving into the traffic lane.

After what felt like six hours, I saw a sign: *Jellystone Park - Camping and Cabins*. Convinced I had reached the outskirts of Estes Park, I was excited—my horrible day was almost over. I stood up out of the saddle and gave it all I had, churning out eight miles per hour before turning into the parking lot and wiping away the snot from my nose.

There was an employee in the parking lot having a smoke.

"Estes Park," I said, not necessarily to him. "I made it!"

"Uh, no," he said. "Estes Park is about five miles north."

I wanted to die.

"Looks like you have gear," the employee said. "We have a campsite available."

"What about food? Any restaurants nearby?"

"Nearest ones are in Estes Park."

I wanted to set up my tent, but I was starving. I stared in the direction of Estes Park like a soldier being redeployed.

"Alright, well I'm going to shoot for Estes Park, then. Thanks."

Five miles took me forty-five minutes. My lungs burned, but at least it was cooler at 7,500 feet.

I stopped at the Estes Park Visitors Center on the west side of Lake Estes to find a campground. I was pointed to the KOA on the northeast side of the lake. This day would not end.

Pedaling along Big Thompson Avenue, I kept a sharp eye out for where I was going to dine.

- McDonald's
- Subway
- Antonio's Real New York Pizza
- Hunters Chophouse

You might think I made a bee-line straight for the Subway, but I was open.

The familiar A-framed office building with three boxed letters—K O A—stood proudly in the shadow of Mount Olympus.

That was a heavy load to assume such a name—Mount Olympus, where the gods of Greece lived. The name Estes Park was less impressive, almost generic like its sole purpose was to sell appealing T-shirts.

"You biking?" the lady at the desk asked as she slid me my registration card.

"Yep."

"Another guy in Site H is biking, too. Just checked in. Are you with him?"

"Really?" I was genuinely surprised. "No, I'm not with him."

I filled out the registration card. A tall, narrow, grey-haired fella in Lycra walked in with a half-eaten peanut butter sandwich in his hand and a smile on his face.

"Do you want to go to dinner with me?" he asked.

"Damn straight," I said, happy to meet a kindred spirit. "Give me five minutes to get my stuff in my campsite."

Another cyclist! Finally, someone to share lonely road stories with. I didn't even shower, just put on the least smelly clothes I had and walked my bike to his tent.

"What are you up for?"

His name was Don. We ended up at a little Mexican place. I would have preferred a steak, potato, salad, and whiskey, but a wet beef burrito, chips and salsa, and a couple of Pacifico *cervezas* did the trick.

The restaurant was staffed by a bunch of foreign work program students. Our waitress was from the Czech Republic. I attempted to flirt, trying to impress her with the only Czech I knew—*jak se máš?* (How are you?)—which did nothing in the way of sealing the deal.

"So, Don, where you headed?"

"I'm just doing an eleven-day ride over most of Colorado's summits."

"Alone? You couldn't get anybody else to go with you?"

"Nope. Couldn't get no one in the nursing home to come with me." He smiled.

Don, the Grey Fox, was seventy-one. If I were to guess, he weighed about 115 pounds wet and stood just under six feet. His Lycra cycling shorts barely clung to his skeletal frame. He told me he had scoliosis and arthritis in both knees.

His mountain bike was a steel Specialized Stumpjumper from the 1980s, complete with plenty of rust and a kickstand.

His panniers were handmade from old canvas newspaper delivery bags and pegboard that he attached to a make-shift bike rack. In them was a sleeping bag, tent, air mattress, rain gear, change of clothes, cold weather gear, and lastly, a pen and notebook for his poetry.

As I poured Cholula all over my burrito, Don told me he had once raced on Team 7-Eleven. The amateur cycling team was started in 1981, with one of its notable teammates being Bob Roll, who later raced with Greg LeMond on the Z Team[45] in 1991. I didn't know if I believed Don, but I didn't question him.

When I was seventy-one, sitting on some park bench in Florida waiting for death to take me, would some youngster believe my tall tale of cycling from Minnesota to California?

While sipping my second beer, Don added to his life's resume with a napkin sketch of the roof-mounted bike rack he designed.

"The roof bike rack was my idea. No one had ever thought of it, but before I could patent it, the idea was stolen from me."

"What, really? If that's true, I'd be pissed."

He smiled and dipped a chip into the salsa.

After dinner, Don wanted to take me to the Stanley Hotel. It was at the hotel where Stephen King was inspired to write *The Shining*. Although the Stanley was not part of the original movie, it was where they filmed the lesser-known, made-for-TV miniseries, which had the blessing of the writer himself, Steven Weber, Rebecca De Mornay, and a bunch of shitty animation. I had no interest in biking up there. I had already visited the Stanley many years before, being an avid fan of horror, ghost stories, and various mysteries of the unknown.

Returning to the KOA, I told Don I was going to start a fire, and he was more than welcome to sit by it and listen to the wood crackle.

---

45 Pro cycling team Greg LeMond joined in 1990 and with whom he won his third and final Tour de France. In 1991, he took seventh and did not finish. In 1994, he retired from a professional cycling career.

The dude in the campsite next to me was already set up. He had been there a few nights already, doing day hikes and making nature photos.

"How far you going tomorrow?" he asked.

"Hot Sulphur Springs."

"You might make Granby, but not Hot Sulphur Springs."

"I'll make it."

"You know, last night a moose was prancing around your campsite, just thought you should know."

Well, shit, man, I thought. *What am I supposed to do if an 859-pound moose comes back to trounce MY designated campsite? Thanks for that thought, neighbor.*

Twenty minutes went by before Don came over. The fire was going strong. There was plenty of kindling scattered about to get the fire started, and I scavenged for some dry wood near the campsite, ignoring the *Do Not Scavenge for Firewood* sign. I hadn't planned on making it a long night, so I constructed a modest, cozy fire to last twenty or thirty minutes.

The sun was now behind the Rocky Mountains, creating an amazing silhouette of the entire range. As the sun dropped, the temperature followed suit, dropping by twenty degrees. Elk bugles echoed through the valley as the fire crackled. I watched the silhouette of the mountains disappear, mountains that I would be atop tomorrow.

Don found a comfortable chunk of a tree to use as a seat. He opened a piece of paper and read me a poem he wrote in Aspen.

Then he looked at me, crumbled up the poem, and shoved it in his fanny pack. He stared at the fire with a grin as if his memories were stored somewhere in the flames.

I watched the sparks reflect in Don's eyes. Embers rose, following their own random trajectory before extinguishing against the night sky.

Don was one of those random sparks born from the fire. As the spark left the flame, he left the safety of home. His life, like these embers, would soon be extinguished. Perhaps that was what he thought about. My spark was rising as well, toward its own end, but nearer to the fire than Don's was.

Him, then me, then those that followed after. My nieces and nephews, still in diapers, still nurtured in the safety of the fire, soon would be sparks, old men and women blinking into darkness.

Don was born in 1930. The Empire State Building was completed when he was just one. When he was six, they finished the Hoover Dam. He lived through the Great Depression. At age eight, he probably heard Orson Welles deliver *War of the Worlds* on the radio. At age eleven, he learned that Japan bombed Pearl Harbor. He was fifteen when World War II ended. When Don was seventeen, Chuck Yeager broke the sound barrier in his X-1 jet. The Korean War broke out when he was twenty—did he fight? JFK, MLK, and Bobby Kennedy assassinations, all happened during his thirties.

His spark had seen a lot in its short journey here on earth.

Don left as the fire turned to coals. I'd never see Don again. Before crawling into the Blue Kazoo, perhaps in Don's honor, I decided to write a poem:

It has come to pass that all
we have seen has been dismissed

It has come to pass that all
we have seen is currently being dismissed

It has come to pass that all
that has been dismissed is being seen

That is when time has found itself

Only to discover a tangled spoked wheel

All at once the rotation starts

I think there was still a little tequila left in me.

CHAPTER 11

DAY TWENTY-ONE

SEPTEMBER 11, 2001

Today's Ride: Estes Park, Colorado – Hot Sulphur Springs, Colorado
Today's Distance: 70 Miles

"I told my pap and mam I was comin' to the mountains to trap and
be a mountain man. Acted like they was gut shot! Sez, son, make
your life go here. Here is where the people is. Them mountains is
for animals and savages. I sez, Mother Gue, the Rocky Mountains is
the marrow of the world. By God, I was right!"

- DEL GUE[46]

I didn't think I slept a wink. I spent the whole night with one eye
open waiting for that damn 859-pound moose to come back to
my campsite.

The sun was still behind the mountains when I woke up. A layer
of frost covered the tent. It was, by far, the coldest morning I'd had
on this trip, somewhere in the thirties, I suspected.

46 A mountain man who befriends Robert Redford's Jeremiah Johnson character in the
movie *Jeremiah Johnson*.

I didn't bother waiting for everything to dry. I had a big day ahead of me and wanted to get an early start, so I shoved my dew-soaked tent and sleeping bag carelessly into my backpack, balanced it out the best I could, strapped it to the rack, and headed for the road.

Walking my bike past the office, a dude sitting in his car rolled down his window. He looked a bit out of it—maybe drunk from the night before. I could faintly hear the news on his radio. After I passed him, he barked at me.

"They just blewed up the World Trade Center!"

Or at least that was what it sounded like he said. I stopped in my tracks. "What?"

"THEY JUST BLEWED UP THE WORLD TRADE CENTER!"

I decided to ignore him. What he was saying didn't make sense, nor was it grammatically accurate.

From the looks of him, it was a surprise that he even knew what the World Trade Center was. Then again, he could have been a former Wall Street trader who had burned out—lost his mind—and ended up living in an old Pontiac in Estes Park. Or maybe he was the antichrist that I heard call into Art Bell.

I rode back toward Main Street to find breakfast—two eggs, hash browns, and heart-stopping sausage gravy.

I passed my Visa to the cashier.

"Oh…" she said. "I'm sorry, the Visa machine ain't working, because of what's happening."

"Because of what's happening?" I asked. "What's happening?"

"Oh, just some sort of accident in New York. They don't know, really. So just cash today, sweetie. Okay?"

Fortunately, I had grabbed some cash in Boulder. I paid and headed west on US Route 34.

It was four miles until I reached the entrance to Rocky Mountain National Park.

Fee for bikes: five dollars.

The park ranger took my cash and pointed on the map at two locations at the top of the pass.

"The upper pass is closed from here to here until 2:00 p.m."

"Til 2:00 p.m., huh? I don't think I'll be there by two."

He looked me up and down. "Yeah, I don't think so either."

It was about 9:00 a.m., and that summit was twenty-four miles and 4,500 feet of climbing away.

After the entrance gate, the road became as smooth as glass and vacant of all vehicles. It was just me, nature, and… out of the mist, two cyclists whizzed passed me as if I was stationary. I didn't know one could go that fast on a bike, self-propelled. They were like gods, but I, too, placed myself in the field of celestial beings, for I had cycled many miles and overcome many things.

They disappeared along the road that snaked upward toward the pass.

What were they doing? Were they just doing a day ride to the top and back? Impossible. But I didn't see any gear to suggest otherwise.

I began my ascent, stopping at every vista overlook to rest and recalculate how long it was going to take me to get to the top at my last recorded speed. My average speed was 3.4 miles per hour, which was about one mile per hour faster than simply walking. I knew this because as I stopped and walked a few times, the computer read 2.3 miles per hour.

The scenery was outstanding. I soaked it all in, which was easy to do at 3.4 miles per hour. For as difficult as this was becoming, I was very happy to be on my bike, enjoying every inch, as opposed to zipping past it all in a car.

About an hour into the park, I heard a voice from behind me. Two more bicyclists soon began to overtake me.

"What's with the pack?" one of them asked as they pulled alongside me.

"I'm biking to California."

"Geez, that's ambitious," the other rider said. He moved in front of me and started drafting.[47]

"Thanks," I said.

The whole idea of me drafting behind him at my speed seemed ridiculous, but I was appreciative of the gesture.

"No problem," he called back. "Have you heard the news?"

"No, not the details. Sounds like something's happening out east, maybe in New York. What's the word?"

"Terrorists!" the other guy shouted.

I was dumbstruck.

"Yep," said the first guy. "Terrorists crashed a plane into the World Trade Center in New York."

"Are you serious?"

"As serious as this climb over the Rocky Mountains." I didn't say anything in response, too busy thinking about what I'd just heard, so he continued, "Well, we'll see you at the top maybe. Where you staying tonight?"

"Hot Sulphur Springs."

"Shoot for Granby. At your pace you won't make Hot Sulphur Springs."

I didn't take offense. My head was spinning. Here I was, in all of nature's grandeur on an epic day, and simultaneously, as a US American, I was under attack.

Perhaps selfish, but I realized there was nothing I could do

47 Two or more cyclists ride in a tight single file line, with the back rider taking advantage of the slipstream created by the front rider.

about New York. I needed to make it to Hot Sulphur Springs, and I was apparently doing a very poor job of that.

Over the next four hours, I pedaled and walked, pedaled and walked.

I was just over halfway when two cyclists, loaded down with gear, riding touring bikes, came within sight. I was on my way to overtaking them, which was a much-needed boost to my ego.

"Where you headed?" I asked.

"To Grand Junction, then we're taking the Amtrak to San Francisco. And you?"

"San Fran."

"How do you plan on crossing the desert?"

"How do I plan on crossing the desert?" I said. "Shit, I don't know. I'm trying to get over these mountains first. Haven't planned out that far. Just want to be in Hot Sulphur Springs tonight."

"You'll never make it to Hot Sulphur Springs," they said. "You should just get to Granby."

"I'll make it!"

"Did you hear that the Pentagon's been hit?"

"Hit with what?"

"A plane crashed into the Pentagon. The world's falling apart, and we're out here riding our bikes."

"I thought it was the World Trade Center?"

"Yep, they were hit first, then the Pentagon. Good luck, we're going to pull over and take a break."

All I could do was hammer on. None of it made any sense. I lacked the ability to even imagine what had happened. I had my own struggle, and it was more real to me than those plane crashes.

An hour later, a sign appeared: *10,500 feet.* Just another 1,800 feet of elevation to get over before the pass.

I was feeling a bit more confident about making it to Hot Sulphur Springs before nightfall. Not that I had any doubt, but I certainly didn't receive any encouragement from the strangers I had come across.

The two color-coordinated bikers who had passed me hours before came whizzing down the mountain at a phenomenal speed. They had either enjoyed a long lunch or rode all the way to the park entrance on the west side, then back up and over. Incredible. I wondered if they had granny gears.

I couldn't wait to start my descent, but for now the road just kept going up and up and up. One more bend, one more false summit. The top seemed unreachable. I could see the top, but the road seemed to stretch, pulling me further away with every pedal stroke.

It was very cold. There were patches of snow scattered about the scree. I was riding the ridge, and as I neared the top, above the tree line, a wind from the west almost blew me off the road.

Another bicyclist was twenty yards ahead, putting on his wind breaker. I wished I had a wind breaker; I was freezing.

"Almost there," he shouted.

Almost there. I hated when people said that. When I ran marathons—or should I say, shuffled them—people would shout,

"You're almost there!" as I was passing mile eight. I wasn't almost there, I had eighteen more miles to go. It was as if they thought we couldn't count.

"Thanks," I shouted back.

"You don't have much further," he said as I got closer. "Are you staying in Granby?"

"Heading to Hot Sulphur Springs."

"Oh, just go to Granby. Hot Sulphur Springs will add another ten miles to your day. You'll never make it."

Fifteen minutes later, I reached Gore Canyon Overlook, where I turned into a parking lot that offered an awesome view and gave me time to catch my breath. The altitude made the breathing part particularly challenging.

Dismounting, I took in the *Never Summer Mountains*, a slight tweak on the Arapaho name *Ni-chebe-chii*, "never no summer."

It was amazing. Hell, I was amazing. I just biked to the top of the Rocky Mountains. A feat of the gods. Closing my eyes, I could hear the chalices clanking as they toasted me in Valhalla.

The sun was heading west fast. I didn't have much time to dil-lydally, so I took one more glance and started walking toward the road with my bike. A tall, thin guy wearing some very weathered motorcycle leathers approached me.

With a smile, he brought your weary hero gifts. He handed me a Heineken and a handful of Wheat Thins. Only a steak from Peter Luger could top this feast.

"You made it!" he said, extending the box of Wheat Thins toward me, inviting me to have more.

"I overtook the pass? Really?" I looked around. Where were the crowds of people to congratulate me, my medal, my T-shirt... the band? I felt robbed. "Thanks. And thank you for the beer and crackers."

"Biking across the country? I used to do that, but I traded my bicycle for a motorcycle."

"I used to ride my motorcycle cross-country, and here I am pedaling," I responded with a smile.

We shared the same taste in motorcycles, it turned out. He had a 1978 BMW R90. My ride was a 1980 BMW R65.

It had been while riding my R65 in the Navajo Nation back in 1995 that I met some dude on a road bike at Four Corners. The magical location was where Colorado, Utah, Arizona, and New Mexico met, where you could overpay for Indian fry bread and Native American souvenirs. He was riding from California to New Jersey. I remembered thinking, *one day I'm going to do an epic bike trip.* And here I was, seven years later, on that very journey—not as far but just as alone.

"Where are you headed?" I asked, grabbing another handful of crackers.

"I'm motorcycling from San Francisco to Lincoln, Nebraska, hitting all the hot springs along the way."

"A hot spring road trip. That's genius!"

In Colorado, there were six well known hot springs. Nevada had one well-established hot spring in Carson City, and there were thirty in California. Nebraska had corn.

"I know." He smiled, drinking his beer. "You staying in Granby tonight?"

"No, Hot Sulphur Springs."

He took a deep breath and looked at his watch. "You probably can make Hot Sulphur, but you gotta leave now. Hand me your empty and be safe."

One mile downhill, I coasted into the Alpine Visitor Center parking lot.

I was freezing, completely unprepared for this temperature. It had been a solid eighty degrees every day since I left Minneapolis, if not warmer, but here at eleven thousand feet, it was maybe forty.

I walked into the visitor center, passed all the tourists flipping thru postcards and unfolding the carefully folded shirts, and headed straight to the cafeteria, where I ordered a sandwich, potato salad, and a large hot chocolate.

The cafeteria had the most spectacular view. It didn't matter if I reached Hot Sulphur Springs anymore, I could sit here the rest of the day. Maybe hide in a broom closet until they locked up and then live in the Alpine Visitor Center, taking a chapter out of *From the Mixed-Up Files of Mrs. Basil E. Frankweiler*, where Claudia and Jamie Kincaid made the Metropolitan Museum of Art in New York their home.

It was getting overcast and, according to the time stamp on my receipt, it was 3:47 p.m. I had forty-eight miles to go, albeit all downhill. At twenty-four miles per hour, I would be in Hot Sulphur Springs before six.

Five guys in their fifties were sitting next to where my bike was locked up.

"Where you headed?" they asked as I approached.

"California," I said, unlocking my bike, trying to dodge them entirely. I had precious little time to make my goal, even if it was all downhill. Anything could happen. I could get a flat tyre or crash on the descent.

"We biked across the country once. Not like how you're doing it. We set up a flatbed trailer with furniture and a bar. Whenever we wanted to take a break, the driver would stop and we could sit on the couch, make a meal, have a cocktail, then start pedaling again whenever we were ready."

"Sounds fun." It honestly sounded genius. "I gotta go, though. Trying to make Hot Sulphur Springs."

"Just go to Granby," they said. "You'll never make Hot Sulphur Springs."

Five rotations on the cranks and gravity did the rest. I was soon at thirty-five miles per hour.

Downhill, I took over the middle of the lane, but it was a bit trickier than I suspected, especially with my gear shifting around the turns at speed. The Topeak rack kept moving side to side as I banked the corners, shifting all my gear whichever way I was leaning. I had to keep reaching back to center the gear in order to keep my balance, which could only be done on the straightaways.

Before the park exit, there were five hairpin curves that were highly influential in convincing me to lower my speed by about a third. Loose gravel and sand were also factors I had to consider as I banked hard on each turn during the descent. Braking with one hand and pushing my gear back to center with the other only proved my handling skills were legendary.

The temperature began to rise, and after the last hairpin, the descent mellowed out. I let go of the brake levers. Twenty miles after leaving the Alpine Visitor Center, I reached the west exit of the Rocky Mountain National Park.

Climbing the Rockies was by far the most physically challenging undertaking I had ever done on a bicycle. From there, I felt I would simply coast to California.

Twenty-five miles to Hot Sulphur Springs, I skirted past Shadow Mountain Lake and Lake Granby without taking a glance... well, maybe one glance. But I was in a race against the sun, which was touching the top of the mountains. It was going to be dark soon.

Reaching US Highway 40, I had my chance to turn left and stay in Granby for the night. Distance: half a mile. Or, I could go right and head for Hot Sulphur Springs. Distance: ten miles

I opted to prove all the naysayers wrong and turned right. I made it to Hot Sulphur Springs in another thirty minutes. The subtle glow of the setting sun was still visible behind the mountains west of me as I reached the sign that read: *Welcome to Hot Sulphur Springs.*

Just beyond the welcome sign was a small blue sign indicating camping to the right. I turned down Grand Avenue. The town of

Hot Sulphur Springs was five streets long. I reached a bridge, which crossed over the Colorado River. From there, a dirt road led me past a campsite where a portable kiosk sign was placed, reading: *TERRORISTS SUCK, FREE BEER.*

I'd return to learn more about that sign, but for now I was headed straight for the eponymous hot springs.

I locked up my bike, hobbled into the entrance, and in exchange for ten dollars, was given a robe, sandals, and access to the springs.

The Ute Indians called this place *big medicine.* There were seven pools to choose from with temperatures ranging from 104 to 126 degrees. The pools were heated by volcanic rock thirty-five thousand feet below.

How they knew what was that far down was above my pay grade. I recalled reading about how the Russians dug 40,230 feet down only to discover it was too hot to keep digging. The project was called the Kola Superdeep Borehole. It took them twenty years to go seven and a half miles. That was an average speed of 23,360 hours per mile. This made my speed over the Rockies today a little more impressive by comparison.

The pool I found to be most relaxing was 110 degrees. Hot springs and sunburn didn't mix very well in the beginning, but I soaked and stared at the clear and starry sky, counting the satellites and watching as shooting stars burned out and disappeared forever.

Twenty-five minutes of soaking and I was ready to learn more about the day's news. It seemed like by returning to the kiosk, I might get caught up on current events.

As I approached the sign, I could see flames from a raging campfire flickering behind it. Two thirty-something guys, one wearing a NASCAR shirt, the other, Hard Rock Cafe Las Vegas, watched me as I walked up. Next to them, a woman wearing a sweatshirt from the University of Louisiana stood by the fire pit with a plastic cup of what I assumed—and would soon find out—was the aforementioned free beer.

An older guy worked at growing the fire, although it was fine on its own, already about three feet high. Two other women approached to refill their plastic cups at a keg.

As I leaned my bike against a nearby tree, one of the women handed me a beer.

"Thanks," I said. "So, what's all this about?"

"You haven't heard?"

"I heard something about a plane crashing in New York and maybe another plane crash at the Pentagon. I haven't had access to a radio or TV."

"They don't know exactly. A bunch of planes where highjacked by Saudis."

"Saudis? Aren't we buddies with the Saudis? Or at least business partners? For oil and stuff?"

"What are you talking about?" the dude in the NASCAR shirt snapped. "Why would we do business with the Saudis? Are you stupid?"

"I'm not stupid," I told him, taking a sip of my beer. "We've been working with the Saudis since the thirties. Shit, we even have a couple of military bases there, I think."

"You don't have a clue what you're talking about," NASCAR continued. "Why would we be friends with the fucking sand n****rs that attacked our country? Explain that to me!"

"I don't know," I told him, honestly. "There is a lot of crazy in this world. In the eighties, the CIA gave Osama Bin Laden and his army weapons and money to fight the Russians in Afghanistan."

"You anti-American or something?"

"Why would me telling you historical facts make me—"

The old guy interrupted, "He's right. We armed Osama Bin Laden and do have bases in Saudi Arabia."

"Have you never heard the phrase, 'The enemy of my enemy is my friend?'" I asked.

NASCAR spit in the fire. "Bullshit. I don't believe you."

"So," I said, eager to change the subject. "I heard one of the tower's collapsed. Is that true?"

"Dude," said Hard Rock Las Vegas, very loudly and speaking very slowly as if I didn't understand English, "they fucking flew planes into the World Trade Center, the Pentagon, and who knows where else." Speaking slower and condescending, "When you fly a plane into a building it falls down!"

I didn't think it would be a good time to bring up that in 1945 a B-25 Mitchell bomber crashed into the Empire State Building, and it didn't collapse.

"Both towers fell," said the woman in the sweatshirt.

"Both towers? I didn't know that."

"Yeah, we're all stuck here. They've closed all the airports, and no one knows for how long," she added.

The thought of all the airports in the country closed was impossible to wrap my head around.

NASCAR decided to continue to share, "If I was president, I would order our military to carpet bomb the entire Middle East. Nuke 'em. Kill all them Muslims, wipe all them camel jockeys off the planet."

I had no response—or none that I thought would make a difference—so I watched as sparks rose from the fire. They hit me differently than they had the night before. Thousands had their spark extinguished before their time, their unique trajectory stolen from them.

"How many people were killed," I asked, not sure I wanted to know the answer. "Do they know?"

"Probably thousands," said the sweatshirt woman. "They were jumping out of the buildings from the top floors."

"Who was jumping out of the building?"

"People who were in their offices and didn't want to burn up."

The old guy had disappeared and returned with a bottle of Woodford Reserve, unopened. He cracked the cap and handed the bottle to me.

I took a gulp and stared at the cap in his hand. The way the night was going, I thought he might as well throw that cap into the fire. We were going to empty the bottle.

"Does anyone have any good news to share?" I asked.

After a bit of silence, the sweatshirt woman proclaimed, "I got married this weekend."

"Really, that's awesome!"

"That's why we're here, for the wedding."

"Hot Sulphur Springs for your wedding? I had never heard of this place until the other day. Why here?"

"Husband is from here."

"Where's your husband?" I asked, looking around. Given the audience, I half expected to see some dude in the woods peeing, puking, or passed out.

"Oh, he's getting drunk with my dad."

I was getting drunk myself. I sipped my beer, eagerly waiting for the whiskey to make it back to me.

The guy working on the fire was a retired forest ranger who was traveling around the country with his wife. She was in the Winnebago reading.

A pickup truck pulled up. Two twenty-something guys jumped out in search of the free beer. They didn't seem to care too much about the terrorists.

In exchange for the beer, they offered up some pot. A lot of pot actually. They packed up a bowl, and each took a hit before passing the pipe around.

"Where did you get so much dope?" I asked.

"Dude, we were road tripping across Nebraska and found this along the road!"

"This is ditch weed?"

"It's way better than your ordinary ditch weed. We're definitely going back to Nebraska!"

I wondered if the kid who picked me up in South Dakota would think this weed was awesome. I found myself briefly wondering where Mike had ended up. Did he make it to Lincoln, or did he just keep on keeping on?

The whiskey found its way back to me, as did the pipe packed with ditch weed.

"So, what do y'all do?" I asked the two horticulturists.

"I have my own business framing houses," said the one who hadn't spoken yet. He was about six inches taller than his friend and looked like a brick wall. "And he works for me."

"We're heading to Grand Junction for a fight club," said the driver of the pickup.

"Do what? You mean like the movie?"

"Yeah, sorta like the movie, only you win money."

"You fight? Who, just anyone?"

"Yeah, you just go up there and fight someone," said the brick wall. "I won seven hundred bucks last week."

"You look like you'd win," I said. "You do this a lot?"

"Every weekend. And I don't always win. Those Mexicans are pretty feisty, takes a lot to knock them down, even the small ones."

"Aren't they all small," the dude wearing the NASCAR shirt said sarcastically.

We all ignored him.

"I live in Rifle, Colorado. Here's my card with my number on it. If you can make it to my house, we'll take you to a fight in Grand Junction," added brick wall.

"Yeah, okay, maybe. It's about 170 miles out of my way, and I'm on my bike."

"Dude, you're biking? Like, on a bicycle?" asked the driver of the pickup

"Yep, this is day nine. Or ten? I started in Estes Park this morning and pedaled over the Rockies."

"Bullshit! You can't ride your bicycle over the Rocky Mountains," NASCAR said. He was drunk and getting a bit lively.

I decided he didn't like me. After a few more pulls from the bottle and a couple of tokes of ditch weed, I decided I didn't care if he liked me or not. It was time to gather my stuff and set up my tent.

Keeping the rain cover off, I stared at the millions of stars twinkling above.

I thought about what the cyclist had said to me earlier. "The world's falling apart and we're out here riding our bikes."

Maybe the world was falling apart, but for now, under the infinite galaxy, I closed my eyes and ignored that possibility.

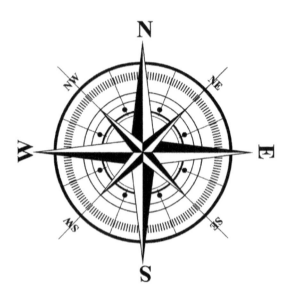

CHAPTER 12

DAY TWENTY-TWO

SEPTEMBER 12, 2001

Today's Ride: Hot Sulphur Springs, Colorado -
Steamboat Springs, Colorado
Today's Distance: 70 Miles

I camped near the retired park ranger's Winnebago. He mentioned before going to bed that I should wake him before I left. I was in no mood to talk and knew if I woke him, it would lead to a cup of coffee and two lost hours of precious daylight. Instead, I quietly packed my gear and headed for Route 40, allowing my retired ranger friend to sleep in.

It was a cool morning. The sun worked its way over the Rocky Mountains, casting wonderful changing shadows across the geography to the west of me.

Route 40 offered a handsome and smooth shoulder. The ride was downhill through Byers Canyon. The Colorado River ran between the road and the Union Pacific Railroad's Moffat Route train tracks, hugging the other side.

In fifteen minutes, I arrived in Parshall, a small town which sat quietly along Route 40. Just three miles south was Williams Fork Reservoir, where legend had it the largest pike ever caught in Colorado found itself on the hook of Dave Van Cleave, weighing in at 30.48 pounds and 44.5 inches long.

Leaving Parshall, I could feel the sun hitting my back, and my whole world thawed.

I crossed over Troublesome Creek, a name given to it by US soldiers who discovered it was a bit *troublesome* to cross when the water was high.

Thirty-five minutes after leaving Parshall, I was sitting at a table at the Grand Old West restaurant, ordering up a bit of the sawmill gravy, *dos huevos*, and hash browns.

A guy wearing cycling clothes, who had been sitting across the restaurant drinking coffee, walked over and asked if he could join me.

"I'm Dale."

"Nice to meet you, Dale. I'm Cory."

"Where are you going?"

"California."

"California, huh? Which way across Nevada you planning on going?"

"I don't really know," I said, pulling out my map. "Route 50 only has four stops, and I don't know about biking on the interstate."

"No problem, Nevada and this portion of Utah"—he pointed from Salt Lake City to Wendover on the map, then followed the interstate with his finger to Reno—"allows you to bike on the interstate. There is really no other way to get across the state."

Nevada seemed so foreign to me. I was shooting for Steamboat Springs, and the next day, I'd shoot for Maybell. That was about all I knew.

The thought of crossing the desert made me a bit apprehensive. Miles of nothing, buried bodies, spirits roaming the aridisols, mutants born from radioactive testing hunting lost travelers and lone cyclists for food and furniture.

Then, there were the distances between towns and lack of facilities on the road. Dots on maps with names that no longer meant anything, ghost towns or perhaps a census error. Towns no longer needed as cars now got hundreds of miles to the tank. I put away the map of Nevada. It was too much to think about. Plus, I still had to get across Colorado.

"Look," I told Dale. "I just want to get to Steamboat Springs today. I'll plan out Nevada when I get to Utah."

Dale was a seasoned cyclist and was currently cycling from Steamboat Springs to Granby with a group. Being the fastest, he was holed up at the Grand Old West having coffee and waiting for his compatriots. I could tell he wanted someone to talk to while he waited, but I had to leave. There were many miles to overtake, and I was but one novice on a bicycle.

He handed me his card, Dean of Coffman Memorial Union at the University of Minnesota.

"I attempted to go to the U of M," I told him, "many moons ago."

"Well, it's not for everyone."

I replied with an agreeable smile and headed off.

The road flattened out, and I settled in at eighteen miles per hour. I came across multiple cyclists heading east—members of Dale's group, I assumed. They were all wearing bright yellow safety vests, one on a recumbent. I understood why Dale was tired of waiting.

As I crossed the dyke at Wolford Mountain Reservoir, eight miles outside of Kremmling, my perfect day began to crumble.

The gloriously smooth, wide shoulder disappeared. Gone. I was forced to ride on the road, which started to gradually ascend.

The heat was brutal, and I became mind-numbingly bored. I wondered about the vacant houses I passed, who had lived there and why. I mean, why here? What did this place offer anyone aside from loneliness and solitude? I suppose those were things which some considered a luxury.

What I didn't know: I was at the beginning of a twenty-one-mile climb to Rabbit Ears Pass, with 2,150 feet of elevation gain ahead of me.

At mile marker 158, the grade increased. This was where the true suffering began. I was condemned to pedal on the shoulderless road, which offered nothing in the way of a safe space to stop and rest. All I could do was grind, sweat, and swear.

I finally reached the last brutal bunch of steep switchbacks, timed perfectly with me running completely out of water.

Those last three miles at four miles per hour took me forty minutes. When I reached the top, the sign read: *East Rabbit Ears Pass.* EAST! What did that mean? Was there a West Rabbit Ears Pass? I pulled out my map and found no wording to indicate another pass. If there was one thing I had learned on this trip, it was that maps lied, but the road did not.

I pedaled west and stopped at the next sign.

Continental Divide

Rabbit Ears Pass

ELEV 9426 FT

Pacific Watershed   Atlantic Watershed

   <————   ————>

Rabbit Ears Pass was the tenth steepest mountain pass in Colorado at 6.8% grade and 9,426 feet, followed by:

9. Wolf Creek Pass - 6.8% at 10,850 feet.

8. Douglas Pass - 7% at 8,268 feet.

7. Vail Pass - 7% at 10,666 feet.

6. Molas Pass - 7%+ at 10,910 feet.

5. Spring Creek Pass - 7.5% at 10,901 feet.

4. McClure Pass - 8% at 8,755 feet.

3. Red Mountain Pass - 8% at 11,018 feet.

2. Hoosier Pass - 8% at 11,541 feet.

1. Slumgullion Pass - 9.4% at 11,361 feet.

Soon after the Continental Divide, I came across what would become my favorite sign in the world—a yellow diamond shape with a truck going downhill. It was time to stop, check the tyres and brakes—it was peanut butter and jelly time!

My emotions went from dread to elation in mere moments. I found myself overtaking my first car. Pedaling was useless, I didn't have enough gear to make it worthwhile, so I rode at the speed of gravity. I smacked my lips, eager to rejuvenate them with water. My main focus was on my speed and keeping my pack from swinging side to side on the turns. I regulated my speed by using my posture. Tucked down, speed increased; straightened up, my body served as an air brake. The brake pads were useless on a downhill like this. Coming to a slow stop in town? No problem. Trying to come to a complete stop doing forty miles per hour plus? Forget about it.

I passed another car, my speed maxing out at forty-five miles per hour. After fifteen minutes, I could see Steamboat Springs in the valley. I couldn't believe this downhill. It was a present—nay, a reward. It was nine miles of bliss.

Steamboat Springs was more beautiful than I remembered. The last time I had been there was in 1995, when some buddies and I decided to road trip to Moab, Utah, to camp and mountain bike.

My choices of places to stay were abundant, but since I spent the last few hours tackling it, I opted to stay at the Rabbit Ears Motel. I checked in, ordered some Chinese, and turned on the TV. I was eager to finally see the events of the prior days.

The replay of the airplanes smashing into the towers wasn't resonating. I watched the event repeat itself for thirty minutes, interrupted only by tone-deaf commercials. The reporters and news commentators talked, but I didn't listen to their words. I couldn't figure out if it was real. How many times had I seen Hollywood blow things up with breathtakingly realistic accuracy? I was more confused than I was upset or angry.

The footage moved from the Twin Towers to a field in Pennsylvania, the wreckage of a smoldering plane, Flight 93, which had crashed in Stonycreek Township. Although the passengers fought with the terrorists to regain control of the plane, in the end, the plane crashed. They played recovered audio of passengers praying, leaving voicemails for loved ones, and planning to fight back. Then they played a voicemail from a man who had been on Flight 175:

"Jules,

This is Brian. Listen, I'm on an airplane that's been hijacked.

If things don't go well, and it's not looking good, I just want you to know that I absolutely love you.

I want you to do good, go have good times—same to my parents and everybody.

I just totally love you… and I'll see you when you get there.

Bye, babe. I hope I call you."

At that moment, it all became real. I sat on the bed and cried. I felt so removed from it all.

The crew, the passengers, the people in the buildings and on the ground, the firefighters… they were all somebody's dad, mom, wife, husband, brother, sister, son, daughter, friend. But they weren't any of those things to me.

CHAPTER 13

DAY TWENTY-THREE

SEPTEMBER 13, 2001

Today's Ride: Steamboat Springs, Colorado - Maybell, Colorado
Today's Distance: 73 Miles

It was 9:15 a.m. when I shut the TV off and shut the door behind me, locking the World Trade Center, the Pentagon, and the field in Stonycreek Township behind me in room twenty-eight at the Rabbit Ears Motel.

In Steamboat Springs, it was just another beautiful morning with the possibility of a scattered shower. The temperature was in the low seventies. Birds chirped, people walked their dogs, and cars traveled north and south along Lincoln Avenue at a gentle speed.

I rode north four blocks to Winona's Restaurant. I locked my bike to a young aspen tree recently planted as a landscape feature, then sat at an available table outside. As I waited for a menu, I locked eyes with a Labrador who was tied to the decorative metal frame of a garbage can. Here was an animal, born to run, chained to an ornate bin on a city sidewalk so its owner could dine. I wondered if the dog even cared.

Winona's Restaurant had a spectacular offering of breakfast which included eight variations of eggs Benedict:

- Crab Benedict

- Philly Jalapeño Benedict

- Bacon, Spinach & Crab Benedict

- Florentine Benedict

- Corned Beef Hash Benedict

- Californian Benedict

- Harvest Benedict

- Traditional Ham Benedict

Although the Philly Jalapeño was my first choice, I went with the Traditional Ham to play it safe. I had more than seventy miles of riding to do. The last thing I wanted was to be haunted by jalapeños fifteen miles from anything.

I couldn't have asked for a more perfect day, but I wasn't excited about getting back on my bike. I would have preferred to spend another night in Steamboat—walking around town, sitting along the Yampa River, having a nice lunch, then later finding a pub to have dinner and some conversation. I should have stayed another day, but I didn't. I finished breakfast, mounted my bike, and headed out on Route 40.

It was 10:45 a.m. when I left Steamboat Springs. Speed limit was now sixty-five miles per hour. I was rocking an average of twenty-one miles per hour thanks to the help of a tailwind and a gradual descent. The distance from Steamboat Springs to Hayden, CO, was twenty-five miles and an elevation drop of 450 feet. The road was a beautiful scenic byway. I was right, it was going to be all downhill to California.

Soon, I found myself riding through a light shower, which turned into a heavy rain. I watched the only cloud in the sky, the one producing the showers, moving northeast. I didn't bother pulling over. I didn't have any rain gear to put on anyway so decided to just ride through. It was my first rain of the trip. Honestly, it was refreshing.

My backpack served as a fender; however, spray from the tyres still covered my face and legs. It was the spray from the cars and—worse yet—the eighteen-wheelers which I could have done without. Fender or no fender, it wasn't long before I was drenched. Being drenched didn't bother me. Actually, it made me appreciate how fortunate I had been. I had biked from Minneapolis to Steamboat

Springs and aside from a few headwinds and some hot days, I'd had very little to contend with when it came to the weather.

Twenty-five minutes later, the cloud passed, and the sun began to dry everything.

I took advantage of the flat stretch of road and decided to run a diagnosis on the drivetrain by shifting through the gears. In the front, I was able to get from the big ring to the middle ring and back to the big ring, but I was no longer able to get into the granny gear. As for the rear, four of the gears worked without skipping. Half my gears were working; my brakes were worn down 75% from when I started, mostly from the last two days of descending. With only about eight hundred miles left, I figured I shouldn't have any problems. I mean, how many gears had I really used since I started this ride?

I spent my time working out the next few days of riding in my head. With the Rocky Mountains and Rabbit Ears Pass—both east and west—behind me, and using nothing more than one major assumption based on the long and relatively flat road I was on, I was certain I would have no more major climbs until I reached the bottom of the Sierra Nevadas.

Hayden was a welcome intermission on the road to Craig. A deserted building designed to look like a Dutch windmill welcomed me. After the windmill, Main Street was five blocks of residential area that then turned into a commercial district. Electric streetlights were designed to replicate old gas lamps. It was a nice touch to spruce up an otherwise dull, one-horse town.

Other than being twelve blocks long, Hayden offered a library. It even had a computer complete with internet and a twenty-minute limit.

It had been four days since I had last checked my emails. I let people know where I was and that I would check in again in a few days when I hoped to arrive in Salt Lake City.

I was hungry but opted to wait to have lunch in Craig. Hayden's only dining options were the Kum & Go or Cenex station. I didn't even bother getting a Gatorade. Craig was only seventeen miles away. I'd be there in an hour.

I was back and forth on whether or not to stay in Craig or press on to Maybell, which was just thirty-one miles further. Even if I stopped to take a roll of pictures, I could be in Maybell by four.

I had begun to notice something after leaving Hot Sulphur Springs on Sept 12, 2001—more American flags on cars and hanging from porches. Almost every sign at banks, schools, and restaurants read: *God Bless America.* Although over the past few days, my contact with people had been limited, there seemed to be a change, a new sense of community. Cars that typically drove past at sixty-five now gave a friendly honk on the horn as if to say, *I'm here for you brother, friend, amigo, comrade. If you need anything, just let me know.* Although the sentiment of the honk was nice, for the most part, the sound of the horn, especially from behind, scared the shit out of me.

When I arrived in Craig, a chain-link fence stretched four blocks, from Emerson to Bellaire Street, which protected the Moffat County Fairgrounds. Red, white, and blue plastic cups were sunk into the links, spelling out *God Bless America, United We Stand*, and *God Bless WTC*. Dozens of American Flags of various sizes hung along the fence, and a few flags were even fashioned with Dixie cups. It was quite a sight. Further down, the Bank of the San Juan sign read: *God Bless WTC*.

I pulled into the Chamber of Commerce on what was now East Victory Way.

Road maps, brochures, and pictures of the area covered the walls. A woman in her fifties sat at the counter.

"How can I help you today?"

"Well, I'm just biking through Craig, heading to Maybell."

"*May Bell*," she corrected me.

"What? Yes, Maybell. Anyway, I have some time here in Craig, is there anything I should see? I'm on a bike, so I want to stay close."

"*May Bell*. Are you interested in cowboys?"

"Yes, very much."

"Well, there is the Museum of Northwest Colorado. It's free and you should visit."

She showed me on the map how to get there.

"Anything else?" she asked.

"Yes, are there hotels and restaurants in Maybell?"

"In *May Bell*?"

"Yes, Maybell."

"It's pronounced *May Bell*, and yes, there are."

"I said Maybell."

"You said Maybell, it's *May Bell*," she said, correcting me again.

"It's spelled M-A-Y-B-E-L-L, correct? Maybell?"

"It's spelled that way, but it's pronounced, *May Bell.*"

"Okay… *May BELL.* Thanks."

"Anytime, have a safe bike ride."

"Oh, one more question. What does WTC mean? I keep seeing it everywhere. God Bless WTC?"

"World Trade Center. You do know we have been attacked by terrorists, right?"

"Yes, yes. I just saw it on the news for the first time, last night. I didn't put it together."

Following her directions, I took East Victory Way to Yampa Avenue, turned right, and a couple of blocks down, on the left corner, stood the old armory, which was now the Museum of Northwest Colorado.

Craig—well, the whole of northwest Colorado—was cowboy country. Craig contained the museum, which for a minimal donation, one was able to wander around. It displayed the great undertaking the cowboys, along with the pioneers, had while roaming and crossing this unforgiving land.

My gear was old, my bike fairly solid, if a bit outdated—these things I thought to be hazards upon departing, well… not really. I would have preferred to have some cool stuff, but one does not need to have the latest and greatest to take a bike trip like this. Upon gazing at the equipment of these travelers of yore, I suddenly felt capable of scaling Everest with the grand tools I was working with.

The road to Maybell was not as impressive as what I had been riding from Steamboat Springs.

The shoulder was wide, but car parts and other obstacles littered my path. Why were there so many car parts? The answer should have been clear, but the last couple of weeks hadn't been about creative thinking. On the other hand, my brain was rested and ready to solve the riddle. I looked to the right. Upon the desert landscape laid an animal skeleton, then another, and another. I was surrounded by hundreds of skeletons. They were sun-bleached, for the most part. Some were still a source of food, with the meat still hanging from the bones. This stretch of road proved to be heavy with roadkill.

I found myself a handsome specimen of a skull and admired it in great detail, then strapped it onto my pack. Another wonderful skull was spotted and attached to my pack. A salvaged length of rope discarded by some passing vehicle soon held my growing vertebra collection—one, two, five, ten, twenty…. I stopped counting and collecting, my rope was full. I was now carrying an impressive collection of animal bones. I felt like a warrior bringing trophies to my tribal leader.

What am I doing collecting skulls and vertebra? I can tell you reader, with 100% honesty, I have no idea. It started with curiosity, then became a small obsession to find the best specimen, which turned into a modest collection of which I ultimately have no use for.

Vultures circled me as I moved west, admiring my newfound collection. At first, I was in awe of them, then the awe wore off and a sense of discomfort set in.

Maybell offered little, but enough to keep all seventy-three of its residents happy. There was the Old Victory Hotel, which was built in 1894 as a hunting lodge, hotel, and stage stop. Originally named the Evans House, it was renamed after World War I, after Victory Way—Highway 40—which ran from coast to coast.

There have been a few famous guests at the old Victory Hotel, such as Teddy Roosevelt and the Astors of New York. Granny Barber said Butch Cassidy and the Sundance Kid stayed a few times as Browns Park[48] was a good hideout.

It was a cozy place with a welcoming front porch but cost more than I was willing to pay. Sure, I could have slept in the same room as Butch and the Sundance Kid, but who was to say they didn't pass out in the same park I was about to camp in. I didn't ask if I could camp in the park, but it turned out none of the seventy-three citizens seemed to mind.

48 Originally a wintering spot for the Ute and Shoshone tribes, would later become a preferred hideout for outlaws.

I put on my cleanest clothes and moseyed on over to Lou's, the only eatery in town. For seven bucks, they offered pork ribs, salad, potatoes, lemonade, and no conversation.

The owner came over with the tab, and I pulled out a ten-dollar bill.

"Anything else I can gitcha?"

"Tell me, do you pronounce it Maybell? Or May Bell?"

"Well, it's spelled Maybell, but pronounced May Bell after the woman it was named after."

"I get it," I told him, a little annoyed that the lady had been right. "Keep the change."

It was dark and getting pretty cold as I walked over to the park. I locked my bike to a picnic table, which I'm sure wasn't necessary. I'd only seen four people since I arrived. It was freezing and I set up my tent quickly, eager to get inside, crawl into my warm sleeping bag, and fall asleep.

UTAH

"People of the Mountains"

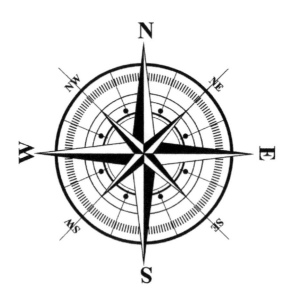

CHAPTER 14

DAY TWENTY-FOUR

SEPTEMBER 14, 2001

Today's Ride: Maybell, Colorado - Roosevelt, Utah
Today's Distance: 119 Miles

On February 1, 1985, the coldest temperature ever recorded in Colorado was in Maybell: -61° Fahrenheit. The temperature when I woke up was only 35°, but it was the coldest I had felt in a long time.

Unzipping the tent door to look outside, I saw that frost covered everything: the grass, my bike, the park benches, the roofs of houses. The only sign of life was smoke rising from the chimneys. I had absolutely no desire to crawl out of my sleeping bag, so I decided to wait for the sun to rise over the mountains and warm things up.

I passed the time by trying to list all the states in the United States. On the first go, I got forty-eight, forgetting Delaware and Alabama. Then, I started in on the capitals. The process beat lying there alone in my tent watching my breath rise in the cold air.

It sounds juvenile but I challenge you to try it.

Once the sun finally started melting the frost, I crawled out of my sleeping bag and exited the tent. Not a soul in sight, the town seemed devoid of life. I filled up the CamelBak bladder and both water bottles using the water pump in the park. Lou's was closed, but the General Store was open. I bought a couple of Snickers bars—one for breakfast and one for later down the road, if I got hungry.

At the edge of town, a sign read: *No Gas 57 Miles.* A second sign soon followed: *Dinosaur - 56 miles.* I anticipated I'd arrive in Dinosaur in a few hours and have a nice lunch once I got there. Fact was, I should have gone back to the General Store and bought a lot more Snickers.

Nothing about this day excited me. The cold, the frost, the lack of a substantial breakfast, the sign telling me I had to bike fifty-seven miles to get to the next town. Depressed and lonely, my mind went dark. I wanted the ride to be over. I wanted someone to talk with.

To add salt to the wound, the ride out of town started with a long climb and a twenty-five-mile-per-hour headwind. The gods were out to get me.

I mustered up every bit of physical energy and mental fortitude I could find to fight the wind and power up the long ascent.

A Snickers bar contains 266 calories. The one I ate for breakfast sure as shit wasn't going to keep me going. But what was I to do? I had no choice but to keep going. Even if I wanted or needed help, no one would know where to find me.

As if the day couldn't get any shittier, the smooth shoulder disappeared and turned into a bone-shattering path loaded with debris—car parts, dead animals, rocks, branches, glass...

It seemed as if I was the only person on this road. I saw no cars, no trucks. I didn't even see an airplane or contrail. The human race could have been completely wiped out, and I wouldn't know it, just like I didn't know what was going on back east a few days ago. As far as I knew, it was just me and the clerk at the Maybell General Store.

My situation could be worse. Juliane Koepcke was seventeen years old when, on Dec 24, 1971, the Lockheed Electra OB-R-941 commercial airliner that she was a passenger on was struck by lightning. The plane immediately broke up in the air. Still strapped to her seat, she fell two miles into the jungle. She survived the fall, with a broken collarbone, a gash on her arm that would eventually become infested with worms, and her right eye swollen shut. She spent ten days alone in the Amazonian rainforest, following a stream, wading through knee-deep water, until eventually she came across a group of fishermen. After two weeks spent recovering, she led a search party back into the jungle to locate the crash, ultimately finding her mother's body.

And here I thought I was having a bad day.

Fighting the headwind, I occasionally took time to stop and stare at the road as it vanished into the horizon. I had been biking for forty minutes and gone only five miles.

I hoped to see a town, a house, a billboard—anything that showed signs of human life—but it was just me and the road and a rather large coyote.

"Coyote?!"

A coyote stood across the road, looking directly at me.

I had some important questions. What was I supposed to do when I came across a coyote? Were they aggressive? Did they attack humans? Were they fast? Could I out-pedal him? Not with this headwind. He could catch me without even having to run.

In the lore of Indigenous Americans, the coyote was many things. To some tribes, it was a hero who created, taught, and helped humans; to others, a warning of negative behaviors like greed and arrogance; still others looked at the coyote as a trickster who lacked wisdom—he got into lots of trouble, but was clever enough to get out of it.

This part of North America was home to the Snake Indians. The Snake Indians were made up of the Northern Paiute, Bannock, and Shoshone. The Bannock believed the coyote came to help and did good deeds for the people.

I looked west and so did the coyote. I looked back at the coyote, he back at me, and then he looked west again and bobbed his head, as if to say, "Let's go."

I started pedaling. The headwind continued; my coyote companion making everything a bit surreal. He was now part of my journey. I put off any thoughts of him being an adversary. He was helping me get through the day.

"You live around here?" I asked the coyote.

The coyote gave no answer.

"You have family? Wife? Kids?"

Still no answer.

"Do you know if there is a good restaurant in Dinosaur? I'm really hungry."

Nothing. He could only be of so much help, I guess.

We moved together along Victory Highway, fighting the wind.

Over the next few miles, I watched him as he pranced over the mounds along the highway. He'd stop and wait for me when he got too far ahead, then would continue once I caught up. I was no longer thinking about the wind or the heat or the bumpy road. I thought about the people who had lived along the Yampa River. Ruins of the Fremont people dated back as far as 1500 BC. Their petroglyphs told their stories. The Snake, Ute, and Navajo came after the Fremont and made the land their new home.

Later came the cowboys. Butch Cassidy and the Wild Bunch, Matt Warner, and Isom Dart all traveled this route when it was just a dusty horse trail, known as the Outlaw Trail.

And as I rode along with my coyote and wistful thoughts, there it was: the all too familiar sound of ninety-five pounds-per-square-inch of air leaving my rear tyre.

The coyote heard it, too. Perhaps the sound startled him, perhaps it let him know dinner was ready. I looked down at my tyre and then at him. His body was turned, now facing me. I felt like perhaps our relationship had changed without my input. I thought back to lunch with my dad, when he asked if I was bringing a gun for protection. Then I looked at my flat tyre.

I took the pack off the bike, flipped the bike upside down to remove the rear wheel, and started removing the tyre and replacing the tube, as fast as I could. I looked up to see what the coyote was doing, but he was gone, vanished. I was relieved but also sad, as I was once again alone.

Fifteen more miles behind me, forty-two miles to Dinosaur, and forty-five miles to the Utah border.

As for the day, Vernal, Utah, was my goal, just seventy-one more miles. None of it really mattered. I didn't care. I wanted to throw my rear wheel as far into the desert as possible, followed by the whole damn bike. Then I would just lay there on the side of the road waiting for somebody—no idea who—to pick me up and drive me directly to Truckee.

In case you, the reader, hadn't noticed. Your hero was very moody.

With a new tube and empty soul, I arrived in Elk Springs. The unincorporated community offered two run-down houses, two hundred yards apart, a dirt road, and a feeling of isolation. I looked around for the coyote, hoping he'd rejoin my journey. No such luck.

The wind eased up after Elk Springs. Although it never totally went away, it changed direction, which offered a bit of a respite.

Eighteen miles after Elk Springs, with just sixteen miles to Dinosaur, another flat tyre.

I dismounted, took off the pack, flipped the bike over, removed the rear wheel, and—for whatever reason—decided to document the event by taking a picture of my dismantled bike on the side of the road in the middle of the desert on a hot September day.

While re-inflating my tyre, a car headed west stopped and asked if I needed help. I was thrilled to actually see someone, but without knowing what else to say, answered with, "No, I'm good."

The exchange was short, but I cherished all twelve seconds of it.

In ten minutes, I was pedaling again.

A couple of miles before reaching the town of Dinosaur, I passed the entrance for Dinosaur National Monument. It was home to eight hundred paleontological sites discovered in 1908, after having been buried for over 150 million years. I told myself I'd return someday, preferably in an air-conditioned car.

I reached Dinosaur around 11:00 a.m. Originally called Artesia, the town changed its name in 1966 to take advantage of its proximity to the monument. It then went a little overboard, renaming its streets: Brachtosaurus Bypass, Diplodicus Drive, Tyranosaurus Street, Ceratosaurus Circle, and Triceratops Terrace.

My options for food were limited: the Loaf 'N Jug or the Highway Bar & Grill. The latter's sign read:

AWESOME FOOD

GREAT BURGERS

THURS TACOS

COLD BEER

All who entered the Highway Bar & Grill—myself included—were tempted by the two-pound hamburger with six pieces of bacon called the Megasaurus Burger. I still had over thirty miles until Vernal and didn't know what gastronomical problems the Megasaurus would create, so I opted for a normal-sized burger, fries, and beer.

Highway 40 in its entirety was referred to as Victory Highway, but after the town of Dinosaur and stopping at Vernal, it was known as Dinosaur Diamond.

Three miles after the town of Dinosaur, I came across a large sign with an image of a Tyrannosaurus Rex running across the desert that read: *Welcome to Utah - Life Elevated.* I stopped to take a photo. How could I not?

Three miles more, I passed Snake John Reef Cutoff Road, after which I started up a slight ascent.

I supposed it was bound to happen. It was the kind of day I was having, but of course, I was completely unprepared for it. Sixteen miles from Vernal, my chain broke.

Temps were in the nineties, with not a car in sight. My chain was broken and bone dry. I never thought I'd need an extra chain or a chain tool for that matter. Hell, I left Minneapolis debating whether or not four tubes were too many. My trusty aluminum steed had regressed from a bicycle to what Baron Karl von Drais called the first generation of bicycles, laufmaschine.[49]

I grabbed the chain, wrapped it around my hand, shoved it in my shirt pocket, and started walking. I figured I would walk up any ascents and coast down the descents. What was another seven hours of travel time?

After walking for fifteen minutes, a white pickup pulled up. It was a company truck, and the driver asked if I needed some help.

"You wouldn't be headed to Vernal?" I asked.

"I live there," said the driver.

"I could use a ride. My chain broke."

"I can take you. There are a couple of bike shops that should be able to help you out. Throw your bike in the back and hop in."

I was covered in dirt and sweat and felt pretty bad jumping in his cab, but he didn't seem to mind.

"How long you been biking?"

"I left Maybell this morning, but I started in Minneapolis a couple of weeks ago."

49 German for *running machine* as it had no pedals.

He seemed neither impressed nor unimpressed.

"What do you do out here?"

"I work for an oil company, sort of a consultant. Make sure the oil rigs are environmentally friendly. Well, as environmentally friendly as they can be for oil rigs."

"Are you from Vernal? Born and raised?"

"No, from Kansas City, Kansas. I met my wife, who is from Vernal, and ended up here."

"Are you Mormon?"

"Hell no, but my wife is. We don't let people know I'm not Mormon, it would be a deal if they found out."

We crossed the Green River, a tributary of the Colorado River, just south of where the Yampa River dumped into it.

Shortly after that, we drove through Naples, Utah, and passed a huge pink smiling dinosaur holding a sign welcoming us to Vernal.

I was hoping the ride would last a bit longer. Aside from a cold beer, I had everything I could possibly want—air conditioning, a comfortable seat, and conversation.

He dropped me at Altitude Cycle off East Main Street. I was able to solve my chain situation in a very short amount of time for a very large amount of money. Turns out you could charge a hefty fee for a chain when you were the only bike shop within a hundred miles.

It was just going on 3:00 p.m. Although my original plan was to stay in Vernal, I decided to press on for Roosevelt. There was plenty of daylight left, and it was just thirty-five miles down the road. If all went well, I would be there in just over two hours.

The ride to Roosevelt started out great, then quickly turned to shit when I was slammed with another headwind, which only intensified. For two and a half hours, I did nothing but pedal and regret leaving Vernal.

Three and a half hours later, I arrived in Roosevelt. Its namesake was President Theodore Roosevelt. As it turned out, one hundred years before—September 14, 1901—Theodore Roosevelt was sworn in as the youngest president of the United States, after President William McKinley was shot and killed by Leon Czolgosz with a .32 caliber revolver which Czolgosz purchased for $4.50.

On the corner of Main and North Eight Hundred East, a giant concrete chief of the Moqui people sat cross-legged, with headdress and peace pipe, looking south, toward what was once his people's land. It was now a Family Dollar.

Behind the concrete chief was the Western Hills Motel, a relic of America's 1960s move westward along Route 40. Although not visually appealing in any way, the price of thirty-five dollars displayed on the kiosk in the parking lot turned that chunk of coal into a diamond. I didn't care that it was a dump. It was cheap and I just wanted to get off my bike and get something to eat.

The town, though small, was spinning with the excitement from the high school football game that was currently in progress. Big trucks and hibachis filled the parking lot of the motel while the sounds of AC/DC filled the air.

I ordered a pizza from the Pizza Hut across the way, ate four slices, took a shower, and passed out on the bed.

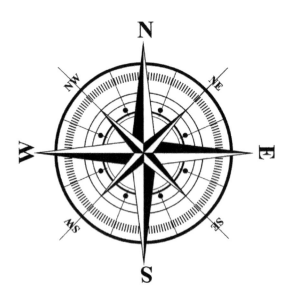

CHAPTER 15

DAY TWENTY-FIVE

SEPTEMBER 15, 2001

Today's Ride: Roosevelt, Utah - Heber City, Utah
Today's Distance: 98 Miles

I woke up around four in the morning, spooning a partially eaten and very dried out pizza. The TV was left on all night, the room hued in blue from the twenty-four-hour news channel. I peed and went back to bed.

At 6:24 a.m., my eyes opened. I spent a few seconds focusing on the emergency exit card tacked to the back of the door. Drool soaked the pillow.

I didn't drink the night before, but I felt like I had a hangover. Totally dehydrated, I picked some dried gunk from my eyes, crawled out of bed, walked over to the bathroom, unwrapped one of the two plastic cups near the leaky, mold-trimmed faucet, and started drinking as much water as I could.

Once again, I found myself naked and disheartened in a motel room, the layout the same as all the others, only with a slightly different smell.

You might be saying to yourself by now, "I get it, my hero likes to mope around naked in cheap motel rooms. Please stop sharing this image!"

Unless of course when you read about this, you envisioned me to have the body and physique of Michelangelo's *David*. In which case, you might look forward to this "word picture" of your hero in the nude at the beginning of each chapter. The reality was, *David* had nothing on me.

The nude morning stroll to and from the bathroom, when I found myself in a motel, was my process. My act of stripping the previous day away before taking on what lay ahead. Preparing for what the day would bring. Would I be gifted with sun, a nice tail wind, and one hundred miles of decent? Or would the gods of wind punish me? Perhaps a day of climbing, rain, and sand burs. I made no assumptions; I just had to make it to the end of the day.

The story required this repetitiveness as it was a real part of the journey. For those of you who might be looking for inspiration to take on the open road alone, it should be noted, the memory of the event was far more romantic than the actual experience, in some cases. Those of you who have done similar trips already know this.

Grabbing a slice of dry, cold pizza, I draped a towel around my waist, opened the door, walked out on the walkway, and leaned against the handrail.

Cans of Coors, Budweiser, and an empty bottle of Jack Daniels littered the parking lot, along with a small pile of dried vomit. I chewed on the slice of pizza then threw the crust out into the lot to join the other remnants of the night before.

It was cool but dry. I changed the channel to CNN, where continued stories of 9/11 played on repeat. I tried to go back to sleep.

Within ten minutes, I was pulling up my crusty black Lycra shorts, yanking my red jersey over my head, gathering and packing my belongings, and heading for the door.

I checked out and clumsily carried my bike down from the second floor to the parking lot, then walked about twenty-five yards over to Sue's Diner. A greasy mom and pop with its original roadside Americana, mid-century décor.

I left my bike near the stands of local newspapers, tourist informational brochures, and coupon books in the vestibule and found a seat at the counter. This allowed me to keep an eye on my bike while I enjoyed my order of two sunny-side-up eggs, crispy hash browns, and a side of sausage gravy. With coffee, of course.

A family of five sat in a booth near the corner window. The father was a doppelganger for Rasputin. The family set an uncomfortable mood in the restaurant. People looked at them sideways, talking under their breath. The kids were filthy and drinking Coke with their eggs, clambering over and under the table. I wondered what their story was. Where did they live? What did he do? I judged them, then ate my eggs.

A woman opened the door for me as I was leaving and she was walking in. She reminded me that God had, in fact, blessed America.

It would turn out to be a slow grind sort of day. To be exact, it would be a 4,800-feet-of-climbing-for-eighty-two-miles sort of slow grind.

A gentle headwind confronted me as I headed southwest out of town on US-191, which ran along Route 40 for a while. The wind only stuck around for ten miles, until I reached Myton.

Myton, known up until 1905 as "The Bridge," offered little reason to stop. As one of Brigham Young's settlement scouts reported when describing the area, "[it] was a vast contiguity of waste. Valueless except for nomadic purposes, hunting grounds for Indians, and to hold the world together."

Pressing on, the road gently ascended toward Duchesne, a town built at the intersection of where the eighteen-mile-long Strawberry River dumped into the Duchesne River.

Originally called Dora, then switched to Theodore in honor of President Theodore Roosevelt, there was soon concern that the town of Theodore would be confused with the town of Roosevelt. The people renamed it again, this time after the river.

I didn't know when my parents decided to name me Cory. I was told the first choice was Anthony, but my mom didn't like the idea of people calling me Tony. So, they went with Cory, a name she decided on after watching *Julia*, a show about a single black mother and her son Corey.

Corey was what my birth certificate originally read until, in 1976, my parents changed it. Corey was crossed out with an asterisk and the new spelling took its place.

That wasn't the only name change in the family. My parents had a collie named Corky. Just before I was born, my parents—much like the people of Theodore—changed Corky's name to Sparky to avoid confusion.

US 191 and US 40 took different directions in Duchesne. US 191 turned south; US 40 continued west. I continued west toward Starvation State Park, with Heber City as my day's end goal.

At Starvation State Park, I found myself fixing another flat and taking in the scenery.

Twenty-five miles and 1,700 feet of climbing later, I reached Fruitland, which was a total let down—no fruit that I could see. I pedaled through the town of Duchesne thinking I would find a place to eat later down the road—a shitty diner would have been fine. Instead, I found only the Big G, a small trading post with two gas pumps. Inside, an old man stood behind a counter reading the paper. He didn't bother to look up when I walked in.

I grabbed a Gatorade and two First Choice Turkey Breast and Cheese sandwiches.

Due to all the jackrabbits in the area, the town of Fruitland was originally called Rabbit Gulch. In 1907, with hopes of enticing the impetuous, developers changed the name to Fruitland, knowing full well fruit could not grow there. Ninety-five years later, the name Fruitland once again drew in a traveler, only to disappoint.

My day continued upward until—fifteen more miles and 1,650 additional feet of elevation gain later—I arrived at a most spectacular site. At 7,612 feet, nestled cozily on a high plateau, sat over one

million acres of water, known as Strawberry Reservoir. I stopped at
a viewpoint and took it in.

The air was much cooler; the breeze was hardly detectable; and
the sun was partially blocked by scattered clouds.

Heber City was just thirty miles away. The road offered a great
shoulder and, for the first time that day, I wasn't climbing. Twelve
miles of wonderfully flat road lay before me until I came across a
sign that read:

SUMMIT 8020 FT

I had reached Daniel's Pass. From there, it was just eighteen
miles to Heber City. All downhill, a descent of 2,400 feet. At twenty-one miles per hour, I coasted all the way into town.

Mac's Motel off South Main Street caught my eye. It was the
cleanest and safest-looking motel I had seen this entire trip. It was
completely redone with new siding and what looked like the original
neon sign, which read: *Welcome to Heber City*.

The receptionist gave me a key to room eight and took forty-two
dollars from me.

The hotel was an L-shaped, one-story structure. All the rooms
were accessible from the parking lot.

Gathering my bike, I approached my room, put the key in, and
tried to turn it. It turned slightly, but the lock didn't disengage. I
tried again and pushed harder on the door as I turned. One more
time, only I put my shoulder into the door to un-wedge it. I looked
around, turned the key, then put my full body into the door. It

opened, ripping off the interior lock and doorjamb. A large piece of wood went flying across the room.

I looked at the key again. It said room eight. I looked at the number on the door. It said nine.

Sheepishly, I closed the door I had just worked so hard to open, looked around to see if anyone had been watching, grabbed my bike, and walked over to room eight. The lock clicked opened. I went inside, turned on the wall-mounted air-conditioning unit, flipped on the TV for some white noise, and laid on the bed. I was hungry but too tired to do anything about it.

Finally, I mustered the strength to walk outside. There were no cars in the parking lot and a Subway just forty meters away. I ordered a foot-long Spicy Italian with a dangerous amount of mayonnaise, then walked over to the hotel office.

"How is everything?" the attendant asked me.

"Just fine, thanks," I replied. "I wanted to tell you—not sure you know this—but the room next to me... room nine, I think..."

"What about it?" he asked.

"Well... it looks like someone broke into it. The door looks like somebody forced it open. Since I don't see any cars in the parking lot, I wanted to mention it to you. Maybe it's nothing."

Feeling like a good Samaritan, I rapped the counter two times with my knuckles, pointed my index finger at the clerk in a friendly finger gun goodbye, and headed back to room eight with my sandwich. I found a *Law and Order* rerun and drifted off to sleep.

Dun dun.

COMMERCIAL BREAK

For those unfamiliar with Subway's Spicy Italian sandwich, it's now time to let you in on what all the fuss is about. Subway describes the sandwich as follows:

"Our Spicy Italian sandwich is a combo of pepperoni and Genoa salami. Pile on cheese, crunchy veggies, and finish it with your favorite sauce. Or don't. Your call."

Now for a more colorful description. Meet Sandwich Artist Joseph Adams, who has taken a few minutes from his busy schedule to share his thoughts about the Spicy Italian.

"You mean the greatest sandwich ever created by man?

Like the works of great artists such as Rembrandt, da Vinci, and Van Gogh, the Spicy is a work of art which is worthy of its own wing in the sandwich Hall of Fame, if one existed.

The monument is one of man's finest achievements.

All hail the Spicy Italian."

I prefer lettuce, jalapeños, spicy mustard, salt & pepper, parmesan cheese, and of course, an unhealthy amount of mayonnaise on my Spicy Italian, all on white bread. The sandwich provided roughly 960 calories, which I could only justify eating at this frequency because of my long days in the bike saddle.

Worsley had his sextant. Alexander the Great had his war elephants. Annie Edson Taylor had her barrel.

Your hero had the Spicy Italian.

CHAPTER 16

DAY TWENTY-SIX

SEPTEMBER 16, 2001

Today's Ride: Heber City, Utah - Salt Lake City, Utah
Today's Distance: 45 Miles

The rebound girlfriend had a friend named Tracy in Salt Lake City who, along with her roommates, offered to host me for a night. I was looking forward to hanging out with other humans, washing my bike clothes in a machine rather than a hotel sink, and making a nice, simple dinner at the house.

I grabbed a donut and some coffee from the "breakfast buffet" Mac's Motel offered in the office, then sat outside on the curb, looking at my map.

Rand McNally highway maps didn't offer any sort of topography. I was trying to decide which way I wanted to go to Salt Lake City. I had Tracy's address and directions to get to her place off I-80.

I had what appeared to be two obvious options.

Option one was to continue north on US 40 until I hit the interstate, then jump on I-80 and high tail it down the Wasatch Range into the very flat city of Salt Lake City. This option appealed to me because I assumed the entire day would either be flat or downhill.

However, I had never biked on the shoulder of an interstate before, so the idea of it caused a hint of concern.

Option two was to head northwest out of Heber City on UT-222 and bike through the Wasatch Mountain State Park, then connect with UT-190 heading west, which would drop me down into Salt Lake City. From there, I would navigate the almost perfect city street grid to get to Tracy's. What concerned me about this was the map said 222 was closed in the winter. This (incorrectly) led me to believe the road was gravel or in poor condition, and that my bike wouldn't handle it well. My other concern was Wasatch Mountain State Park, which drummed up visions of lots of climbing. That wasn't something I was interested in.

I went with option one.

The first nine miles of my day were spent slowly grinding up nine hundred feet of elevation, north on US 40, until I reached Jordanelle State Park.

It was 10:36 a.m. Salt Lake City was just thirty-four miles away. The next two miles were another five hundred feet of climbing, then it was downhill to I-80.

On the bridge where US 40 crossed over I-80, I stopped. Cars, trucks, motorcycles, vans, and buses were all buzzing under me at speeds clearly exceeding the legal limit of seventy-five miles per hour.

The shoulder looked spacious enough from the bridge, but would it stay that way? Was there gravel and glass and other debris littered along the way that I couldn't see from here. Shredded semi tyres, random plastic bumpers, road kill....

I pedaled north, turned left down the on-ramp, and started down along Eisenhower's great legacy.

It wasn't so bad. All in all, the traffic was better than I had anticipated. The shoulder was wide enough to give a comfortable distance between me and the eighteen-wheelers. I coasted into Salt Lake City maintaining an average speed of thirty-five miles per hour, as it was mostly downhill. A total of 2,100 feet of descent over twenty-two miles. Debris and roadkill? Nonexistent.

I exited south on Seven Hundred East.

I passed the Bicycle Center, a small bike shop, then took a left on Wilmington Avenue, right on Six Hundred East, and left again on Elm Avenue. Midway down that block was my home for the night.

It wasn't even noon. I found a Jimmy Johns and ordered the number five—the Vito—the closest I could find to the Spicy Italian. The Vito was stacked with salami, capicola, and provolone. Add onion, lettuce, tomato, oil and vinegar, and dried herbs, and, I had to say, Subway, you'd gotten yourself some solid competition. I took my Vito back to Tracy's, plopped myself down on her front porch, and dug in. My only regret was that I didn't buy two sandwiches.

Tracy pulled up a few hours later. At first, she seemed a bit confused at the site of a stranger sitting on her porch, but she soon smiled, stepped out of her VW Passat, and warmly said, "I love that you made yourself comfortable! Welcome to Salt Lake City."

She was just returning from camping on Antelope Island.

"You ever been there before?" she asked.

"Never even heard of it."

Antelope Island was a two-hour drive north from Salt Lake City. It sat on the east side of the Great Salt Lake and was chock full of wildlife. Over five hundred bison, bighorn sheep, mule deer, coyotes, bobcats, bald eagles, and—of course—pronghorn called it home. While exploring the area in 1845, Kit Carson and John Frémont came across and shot a pronghorn. In gratitude, they named the place Antelope Island.

I stored Antelope Island in the back of my mind as a place to one day visit. For now, I just wanted to take a shower.

Tracy's roommates arrived just after six. Everyone seemed checked out. We talked a little bit about my trip as we prepared dinner. Nothing about the 9/11 attacks came up, which surprised me. I didn't want to open that door, though. I wanted to eat.

We made tacos. Rather than go the traditional route, I opted to fill a big bowl with ground beef and shovel it down using corn chips.

We grouped into the small living room decorated with non-matching furniture and a TV too big for the space. They put on *Band of Brothers* and passed around a bong. I drifted off to the digitally enhanced sounds of World War II, clean and full.

CHAPTER 17

DAY TWENTY-SEVEN

SEPTEMBER 17, 2001

Today's Ride: Salt Lake City, Utah - Wendover, Nevada
Today's Distance: 124 Miles

"Indians scattered on dawn's highway bleeding; Ghosts crowd the
young child's fragile eggshell mind."

- JIM MORRISON

I had no idea how I planned on crossing Nevada. Aside from the
conversation I'd had with the dean outside Hot Sulphur Springs,
I hadn't given it much thought. I recalled Mr. Dean telling me that I
could bike on the interstate from Salt Lake City to Reno.

There were only two ways across Nevada: I-80 and Route 50.

Route 50 crossed the United States, starting in Ocean City,
Maryland, and ending in Sacramento, California. The portion in
Nevada was referred to as "the Loneliest Road in America."

Route 50 didn't appeal to me. My concern was that if something
happened, I would have a far better chance of getting picked up off
the interstate than I would off the loneliest road.

The other deciding factor was, by adding up the mileage segments, taking the interstate was 520 miles, versus 603 miles by Route 50. That was a whole extra day of riding.

When I woke up at Tracy's, everyone was already gone for work. The note said to just pull the door shut as I left.

With everything loaded and no real sense of which way I was going to go, I biked into downtown and found a coffee shop. I ordered a latte and a bagel, then studied the map again. I made my decision, paid my bill, and started heading west toward the Great Salt Lake.

The biggest flaw in my plan that day was my timing. When my receipt came, it was timestamped 12:53 p.m. A bit of a late start on a normal day. But this was to be my longest-miles day.

An hour and half later, I arrived at the Saltair, perched on the shore of the Great Salt Lake. The first Saltair was completed in 1893, known as the Coney Island of the West. In 1925, a fire destroyed most of the pavilion. Rebuilt, the Saltair caught fire again in 1931 and sat empty until 1981. It was rebuilt fifty years after the second fire, and life soon returned… then disappeared. Upon my visit, the only vendor was a salt water taffy shop surrounded by the smell of rotten eggs. There were many theories as to why the Salt Lake smelled so bad. Some said brine shrimp, some said wetlands, some said it was just the salt, and some said it was all the garbage dumped into it.

The sun was high in the sky. I headed west on I-80 and turned off on Exit 99 toward the TA Station. It appeared to be my last opportunity for food or water before setting out across one hundred miles of the Great Salt Lake Desert. I walked over to the pay phone, sunk $1.50 in quarters into it, called my dad, and left a message on the answering machine.

"Dad, I'm heading out across the desert. It's a hundred miles to Wendover. I will call you when I get there. If you don't hear from me by midnight, tell the police I was heading west on a blue bike with a yellow backpack. I'm wearing black shorts and a dark red jersey. They should be looking in the ditch on the north side of Interstate 80."

I'm sure my dad's hair turned a lighter shade of grey after hearing that message.

I loaded up on three Snickers bars and two bottles of Gatorade and headed west, chasing the previously mentioned and seemingly never-ending vanishing point.

I guessed it was past two when I left the gas station, but it was, in fact, closer to four. I had no idea. The sun was high… high enough.

After a couple of hours of riding at an average speed of eight miles per hour, it was becoming abundantly clear that I was going to be riding in the dark. But I was optimistic. I thought that somehow, I would be able to overcome sixty miles in an hour and forty-five minutes.

My fear of riding along the shoulder of an interstate with vehicles screaming past me at ninety miles per hour was starting to become a little more justified. I watched as the sun kissed the tops of the Silver Island Mountain Range and pedaled faster. The darkness was catching up to me. The lights of speeding vehicles cast my shadow in front of me.

I stared at the horizon and the song "Mr. Siegal" by Tom Waits echoed in my head.

♫ *How do the angels get to sleep when the*
devil leaves his porchlight on. ♫

Wendover was the devil's porchlight, and I couldn't wait to get there.

The upside of this long stretch of wasteland was it was flat, and the shoulder was wide.

I arrived at *Metaphor: The Tree of Utah,* an eighty-seven-foot concrete sculpture by Karl Momen placed in the middle of the Bonneville Salt Flats, twenty-five miles east of the Nevada border. Dedicated in 1986, it was said to be "A hymn to our universe whose glory and dimension is beyond all myth and imagination."

It was dark. Wendover glowed behind the silhouetted buttes, but twenty-eight miles of treacherous shoulder still lay in front of me.

All was not lost—your hero had a new, untested, handlebar-mounted light, a gift from the rebound girlfriend. It ran off four AA batteries and snapped easily onto my handlebars. Armed with this powerful tool, I was ready to take on the next two hours of night.

I switched on the light. Nothing seemed to happen. I put my hand in front of it to see if it worked, and a dim yellowish beam hit (rather, tapped) my hand. It was evident that the light was a piece of shit.

It was a new moon, so I couldn't even count on nature for a light. The glow of Wendover and the salt flats were all I could make out until a vehicle came up from behind, illuminating the shoulder enough to allow me to avoid remnants of blown tyres. But I didn't always avoid them. The first massive piece of discarded tyre I hit nearly launched me over my handlebars.

The dark was not just physically treacherous. At some point, things started getting weird. I think it was when the three little grey aliens began running alongside me. They were on the other side of the ditch on the salt flats. I could see them running with me out of the corner of my eye. Although only three feet high, their short little legs propelled them forward at an impressive speed. They were always looking at me with their big, black, oval eyes and oversized heads. They spoke in gibberish—a high-pitched mumbling. When I turned to catch a glimpse of them, they would disappear, blending into the vast wasteland. I'd search the salt flat, then when I was certain it was just a hallucination, I would turn my head forward and they would return. I tried to pedal faster. It was only a matter of time before the mothership would arrive and snatch me up.

Inside the ship, I awoke floating in a sort of sensory deprivation pod filled with an odorless thick blue glowing liquid. Suddenly I was flushed through a network of flexible, sponge-like tubes. My trajectory did not adhere to the science of gravity. I went up and down, sideways and whichways and upside down until the tubes delivered me to the exam room where I found myself surrounded by the grey beings. They hovered around me, speaking that familiar gibberish I heard along the salt flats. The "surgeon" moved on with the process. My body stiff, in a state of rigor mortis, was floating. The light became blinding, I blinked and then saw Exit 410. It was tense, avoiding highway debris and alien abduction. Anal probed, chip implanted, memory scrubbed, and back on my bike as if nothing had happened, but I finally arrived at the blinding lit up city of Wendover, taking the first exit after the border. A Chevron station that served as a truck stop was using half of Nevada's energy to light its enormous parking lot. The Beatles' "Yellow Submarine" played over a series of megaphones. This song had some sort of meaning for this exact moment, but I couldn't peg it.

The Red Garter Hotel & Casino advertised rooms for thirty-five a night with breakfast. Without an ounce of hesitation, I walked into the lobby, pulling my bike along with me, and dropped down my credit card at the reception desk.

"I want a room for tonight and tomorrow."

Mentally, I was fried—avoiding alien abduction was taxing. I dropped another $1.50 worth of quarters into the payphone in the lobby. Dad's answering machine picked up.

"Dad, I'm in Wendover."

Hanging up the phone, I pushed my bike to the elevator.

In my room, the clock read: 11:45 p.m.

I stripped off all my clothes, unwrapped the plastic from the plastic cup, cranked the AC, drank four cups of water, and passed out on the bed.

Cory: 1
Aliens: ?

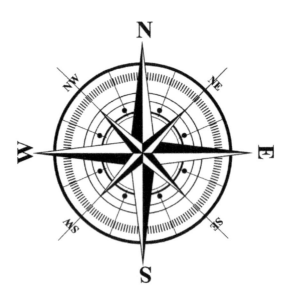

NEVADA

"Covered in Snow"

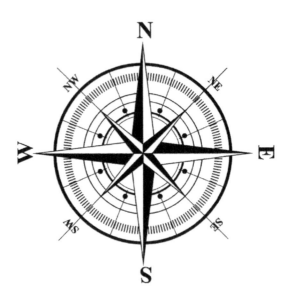

CHAPTER 18

DAY TWENTY-EIGHT

SEPTEMBER 18, 2001

Today's Ride: Wendover, Nevada - Rest Day
Today's Distance: 3 Miles

An attempt had clearly been made, with the help of some super-powerful, industrial-grade chemical, to eliminate the stale smell of years of cigarette smoke. I hadn't noticed the smell the night before.

I didn't notice much when I arrived, except the bed and air conditioning, which I had set to a freezing sixty-five degrees. I woke up to a dry throat and a nosebleed coming on.

I filled a cup with water and walked across the room to open the shades. Outside my window was the desert. Wendover offered more by night than by day. I checked the sky for UFOs. White vans were no longer a concern. I then checked myself in the mirror for marks that would indicate the location of the alien implant.

Unloading my pack, I dug out some clothes, slid on my T-shirt, shorts, and sandals, grabbed my bike, and ventured out in search of a library and a grocery store.

The library was a small, simple building with one computer. I checked in, read some emails, sent out a quick update as to my whereabouts, and searched for any news in the Wendover area reporting UFO sightings last night. The most recent reported UFO sighting in Wendover was in 1998.

There was a Smith's on Wendover Boulevard. I entered the parking lot in a full-on sprint. Why I did that, I had no idea, but I did. As I approached the entrance, I pulled the rear brake lever skidding a solid four feet BMX-style. The braking action snapped a spoke in the process.

The rear wheel immediately went out of true and rubbed against the left brake pad, coming to a full stop. Upon assessing the damage, I saw that the wheel was off a solid inch. I lifted the brake release lever, which opened the brake wider. It was designed to help take off and put on the wheel, but in this case, it kept the rotating wheel from rubbing against the brake pad.

I locked the bike, bought some groceries, and kept my eye open for a bike spoke. Perhaps I'd find one nestled in the cold cuts.

Leaving the parking lot, the bike wobbled dramatically with each rotation. I lost all confidence in the structural integrity of the rear wheel and feared that I was stranded on the island of Wendover.

Thirty years from now, some young kid biking cross-country would mosey into my half-empty bike shop, The Broken Spoke. He'd ask me how I ended up in Wendover while placing his purchase of tubes and tyre irons on the counter. Pointing at my Specialized Allez mounted on the wall behind the cash register, I'd say, "Well son, back in 2001, I was biking to California, on that very bike. I busted a spoke and found myself stranded here in Wendover. We didn't have a bike shop back then. Stranded I was, after breaking a spoke right down the street from here. Just there where the old Smith's grocery store used to be. Course now, it's a teleportation site for all the old folks in Salt Lake City to come out and gamble all their hard-earned Bitcoins away. With no hope of a spoke to somehow magically appear, I took the money I had left from my trip, bought this little shack, and filled it with bike parts. Never did order myself a spoke. Just couldn't bring myself to do it. Oh, I suppose I could have hitched a ride out of this godforsaken place, but I met this desert flower at the craps table, she was serving cocktails. The casino stole the rest of my money, but she stole my heart... her name is Jazmin. She's Hungarian and had her own Airstream a mile north of town. It wasn't long until I moved in, we married, she got her green card, and here I am thirty years later. Me, Jazmin, and my bike with a broken spoke."

(The aliens would continue to check in.)

Something I'd always wanted to learn was how to build a wheel. I once went so far as to buy an old rear wheel for a few bucks, bought a spoke wrench too, and took the time to remove all the spokes and nipples—the structure and foundation of a wheel. I laid them out, starting with the first spoke, then the second. Not knowing the first thing about building a wheel, it wasn't until the fifth spoke that I realized that they were two different lengths, as the hub that came with this wheel had two different diameters.

I gave up on that project and went for a bike ride. I decided that if I was to learn how to build a wheel, I'd just be taking work away from my local bike mechanic. I was being a good citizen, really.

I looked at the map of Nevada, the next major town was Elko—109 miles west. There was no guarantee of a bike shop.

CHAPTER 19

DAY TWENTY-NINE

SEPTEMBER 19, 2001

Today's Ride: Wendover, Nevada - Elko, Nevada
Today's Distance: 109 Miles

After spending far too much time hanging out at the Red Garter, I loaded the bike and pushed it out to the main exit of the hotel. The bike wobbled the whole way. I was not optimistic about the day's outcome.

Before me laid 109 miles of wide shoulder, which would lead me straight to Elko. Below me was an extremely out of true rear wheel verging on collapse.

It was 8:00 a.m., no wind to speak of, and a brisk forty-five degrees.

I checked the tyre pressure. Both tyres required about eight pounds more per square inch.

I then carefully strapped the backpack to the bike rack. It wasn't like strapping the pack on carefully made a difference. Still, I felt like I was saddling an ill-tempered horse. The nicer I was to it, the less likely it would buck me off—maybe.

It was time to get back on the bike—nice, slow, and gentle, so as not to frighten the beast.

I eased carefully into the saddle and made my first pedal stroke. The bike wobbled. The faster I pedaled, the more vicious the wobble. It was only a matter of time until the rear wheel completely fell apart. I spent the first hour of my ride anticipating a fall, my head slamming onto the ground. For the first time on this trip, I regretted leaving my helmet back in Minnesota.

Eleven miles outside of Wendover, I took Exit 398 toward the Pilot Peak historical marker. To me, it was just another indistinguishable mountain. To the tens of thousands of pioneers traveling along the Emigrant Trail, it marked the end of the crossing of the Great Salt Desert.

It occurred to me that, by a simple written description, perhaps just a sketch on some parchment, these pioneers where somehow able to recognize this one peak, Pilot Peak, among so many others in the middle of the desert. Astonishingly, really. Perhaps, along with wagon ruts, someone kindly left a sign.

Choosing to ignore my rear wheel, I pressed on. After eleven miles, I was impressed that the wheel had held together. Ninety-eight miles to Elko.

I approached my first Nevada climb. It was 1,400 feet, up to and over the Silver Zone Pass, which cut through the Toano Range.

At the top of any climb, there was always a feeling of satisfaction. In a perfect world, you would be rewarded with a handsome and speedy descent. I embraced it, without considering my wobbly rear wheel. Over the next three miles, my odometer reached twenty-two miles per hour, then continued up to thirty.

The rear of the bike started wobbling out of control. I squeezed the front brake hard to slow down but not so hard to send me ass over teakettle.[50] The bike slowed only slightly, so I decided to let it ride. If the wheel gave way, and this horse wanted to buck me off, I would have the scars to prove it.

The descent came to an end, and the rear wheel held together. I chalked it up to amazing engineering and a sprinkle of desert magic.

If one were to make a napkin sketch of a bike wheel, it was astonishingly simple. Draw a few circles with some crisscross lines that start from the outside and move inward. Rubber tyre, tube, rim, spokes, and hub. The science behind it was simply complex. The bigger the diameter of the wheel the more centrifugal force was generated and the faster you would go. The spokes, like that of a spider web, were laced in a way where the tension of the spokes pulled away from each other giving the wheel its strength.

The downside, and relevant to my current situation, was when a spoke failed. It put more stress on the remaining spokes, potentially causing a domino effect of failure leading to a collapse of the entire wheel.

An event I expected to happen with great anticipation!

At twelve miles per hour, I wobbled ever closer to Elko with my structurally failing rear wheel.

50 Going over your handlebars.

A bridge, which crossed over the defunct Nevada Northern Railway, was worthy of a photo. The ties and steel overtaken by weeds, a reflection of our post-apocalyptic future. Man overtook the planet, then the planet overtook man.

The tracks led south to an old Western Pacific Railroad construction camp. The first building erected was a bar. A sign was placed with an arrow that read: *To Bar.*

The railroad officials, lacking creativity, called the town Tobar, which now sat alone and abandoned in the vast desert of Nevada. It was destroyed by greed, drought, jackrabbits, and on June 19, 1969, a railroad car full of bombs headed to Vietnam exploded, putting an end to Tobar once and for all.

Exit 378 was the turn off for Oasis. Three abandoned buildings marked the exit, two of which had *FOR SALE* signs.

The next five miles were a 1,170-foot climb up to Pequop Summit Rest area. A skeleton of a rest area, it offered a view of the Pequop Mountains and a single porta potty.

A 1,300-foot descent dropped me back down into the Great Basin, the third largest endorheic basin[51] in the world. It was quiet—even the interstate was lightly traveled.

The wind offered a subtle gust, but nothing strong enough to affect my progress.

In the vast emptiness, lurking in the invisible shadows of the desert, pygmy rabbits foraged the sagebrush, while the coyotes foraged for the pygmy rabbits. Roadrunners chased lizards, while the rattlesnakes tanned. A group of deer pranced along the cracked earth, and bees played with flowers. The wind whispered the songs of the ancients, and prisoners raked the grounds between the chain-link fence and prison.

Just ahead was a sign:

PRISON AREA - DO NOT PICK UP HITCHHIKERS.

---

51 A natural basin with no outflow to exterior bodies of water which creates seasonal lakes or swamps.

Wells Conservation Camp appeared. It was a minimum-security prison whose inmates helped fight wildfires, worked on highway beautification projects, and assisted senior citizens.

Two prisoners stopped their yard work and waved at me. Probably wondered what the hell I was doing out in the middle of nowhere on a bicycle. What got you a minimum-security stint? Seemed almost relaxing. How did I sign up? Take a break from the bike, the desert… from life. Just shut it all down and let someone else think for me for a while. Play cards with like-minded criminal buddies, planning our next caper. Then it'd be off to do some yard work. Wardrobe remained the same. "Three hots and a cot," as the hobos would say. What were Friday nights like in a minimum-security prison? I imagined the movie selection was more than just *Internal Affairs*.

Humboldt Wells became a station along the Union Pacific Railroad, complete with a saloon and a Wells Fargo office.

In 1877, a fire broke out in town. A telegraph went out for help: *Wells is burning*. Since then, the town has been known as Wells.

I exited at 352A and stopped at the Love's truck stop for a brief reprieve. I couldn't believe my rear wheel was still intact and worried that stopping might break my streak of good luck.

Just keep on keeping on.

What if, after I finished my Gatorade and Deli Express turkey and cheese sandwich, the rear wheel didn't want to start turning again? With fifty-nine miles completed for the day, I was just over halfway to Elko. It had taken me about six hours, averaging twelve miles per hour. With the sun setting before seven, I had only five hours of light and fifty more miles to go.

At 6:45 p.m., I wobbled into the city of Elko. The sun provided a final gasp of light as it sunk below the mountains. Vehicles on the highway had all switched on their headlights. I was happy to be off the interstate. I locked in on my home for the night: the High Desert Inn Elko, boasting a forty-five dollar rate.

Entering my second-floor room at the Inn, I found a small phonebook in the nightstand and opened it to Bike Shops. Turns out Elko—population 16,780—had a bike shop: T-Rix, located just one mile away.

I decided to wait until morning to visit the shop. I had a shorter day and would have more time to hang out at the shop. If T-Rix couldn't fix my rear wheel, I felt confident I could still kick out the seventy-two miles to Battle Mountain in five hours.

Part of the California Trail, the town of Elko didn't exist until 1868, when it served as a basecamp for the workers along the Transcontinental Railway.

Legend had it that Charles Crocker, a railroad executive, chose the town's name because he felt it sounded like the name of a railroad. Others said he liked elk and simply added the "o" for emphasis...like *daddy-o*! The third theory was that the name was Shoshone and meant *white woman*.

Whatever the truth was, Elko's tent town consisted of miners, railroad workers, and gamblers. In 1869, the motto of Elko was: "The best government is the least government." A newcomer to Elko wrote: *There were all sorts of games and vices in progress and only two men were killed the day I arrived.*

I ordered Chinese takeout and turned on the news. It occurred to me while dipping my egg roll into hot mustard that I had only five days left until I arrived in Truckee.

CHAPTER 20

DAY THIRTY

SEPTEMBER 20, 2001

Today's Ride: Elko, Nevada - Battle Mountain, Nevada
Today's Distance: 70 Miles

B y nine-thirty, I was out the door and walking my bike to T-Rix. "Good Morning," the clerk said cheerily, as he restocked helmets.

"Hey," I said, optimistic, but not exactly cheery. "So, I broke a spoke back in Wendover two days ago. Unfortunately, there are no bike shops there. I decided to continue westward instead of returning to Salt Lake City and, as luck would have it, Elko has a bike shop. Here you are."

"Yup, here I am."

He took one look at my rear wheel and laughed. "You biked from Wendover on that rear wheel in that condition? Loaded with gear?"

"Yep, painfully slow. Took me about eleven hours."

"You know this bike isn't designed to carry a heavy load, right?"

"Yes, but it's all I have. It's taken me all the way from Minneapolis. Any chance you can at least make it so the rear wheel looks true? I just need to get to Truckee."

"I don't know, this wheel might be shot."

"I know the smart play would be to buy a new rear wheel, but I just need this bike to get me another few hundred miles. Worst case is the wheel just crumbles, and I hitch the rest of the way."

I understood that any one of the other spokes, if not all, could fail at any time. I had 303 miles to the California state line. I was so close.

"I can get it true again, but all these spokes are compromised."

Thirty minutes later, the wheel spun true, and I was out the door.

"Hey," the clerk called out as I was leaving, "visit White King before you leave town. He's at the Commercial Casino off Fourth Street, downtown." He chuckled, "You've got to see him."

I didn't ask who or what White King was, but I was curious, and time was on my side. I headed down Idaho Street. The bike felt brand new; the rear wheel spun perfectly.

If you ever found yourself in Elko, Nevada, visit White King. The experience was similar to visiting the World's Largest Ball of Twine. You'd be glad you did it, but it was not a life-changing event.

White King's claim was that he was the world's largest polar bear. Thanks to a challenge brought forth in 1957, he was now the world's largest *stuffed* polar bear. He stood at ten feet, four inches in a glass case on the corner of Idaho and Fourth Street, in the middle of the Nevada desert, at a coffee shop in Elko's Commercial Hotel and Casino.

Previously, White King could be found roaming the Arctic Circle, eating seals, walrus, and beluga whales. Polar bear vs. beluga whale—that'd be an event I would love to see.

Hunter S. Thompson claimed he kept a drunk (future) Supreme Court Justice, Clarence Thomas, from shooting the stuffed White King. Thomas allegedly shouted, "I've had enough of this goddamn beast. It doesn't belong here. We should blow its head off."

This begged the obvious question: What were Hunter S. Thompson and Clarence Thomas doing together in Elko, Nevada. Perhaps Clarence did, in fact, decide to, "Buy the ticket, take the ride."

Your hero was pro-gun and pro-hunting when the cause was valid—food, animal management. But to travel to the Arctic Circle to shoot a bear from a hundred yards away for the sake of displaying it? Eh… Though, I did start to wonder what polar bear tasted like.

From the White King, I rode out to the highway, which cut past the Elko Airport. A plaque was mounted near the entrance of the runway.

ELKO AIRPORT

TERMINUS OF THE FIRST COMMERCIAL AIR MAIL ROUTE

ON APRIL 6, 1926, VARNEY AIR LINES PILOT LEON CUDDEBACK, CARRYING ONE BAG OF MAIL, LANDED HIS TINY CURTISS SWALLOW BIPLANE AT ELKO, NEVADA, COMPLETING THE FIRST SCHEDULED AIR MAIL RUN IN THE UNITED STATES.

THE SINGLE ENGINE 90 H.P. AIRCRAFT HAD TAKEN OFF FROM PASCO, WASHINGTON, STOPPED AT BOISE, IDAHO FOR FUEL AND MAIL, THEN COMPLETED THE 460 MILE FLIGHT TO ELKO. THE VARNEY CONTRACT WAS AWARDED OCTOBER 27, 1925, AT A RATE OF 6¢ AN OUNCE. VARNEY SOLD TO BOEING WHICH MERGED WITH UNITED AIRLINES IN 1931.

STATE HISTORICAL MARKER NO.207
NEVADA STATE PARK SYSTEM
NORTHEASTERN NEVADA HISTORICAL SOCIETY

Hopping on I-80, the road offered a kind shoulder, free of debris, and a nice flat approach. My biggest climb for the day; the on-ramp to I-80. Upon reaching the 'summit,' I settled into a nice cadence averaging about eighteen miles per hour.

Sixteen miles west of Elko was the Carlin Tunnel. Approaching I could only see the opening on the east face of the mountain—actually, four holes penetrated the mountain: one for westbound traffic, one for eastbound, and two for the railway built by competing rail lines, Southern Pacific and Western Pacific, in the early 1900s.

The exit could be five miles away, maybe ten. Orange cones directed vehicles into the left lane. Perhaps for maintenance, perhaps a ruse to slow traffic down in the middle of Nevada. Perhaps a bit more of the desert magic, as this gave me full use of the right lane and offered clear passage through. The tunnel offered absolutely no shoulder. It turned out the tunnel was just 1,600 feet.

When Eisenhower's legacy was being built in the seventies, it was a shipbuilder that won the contract for the east and west-bound tunnels. Subbing out the excavating, the design Lockheed Shipbuilding Company used to support the tunnel required a complex steel arch. To solve this, they simply built a steel hull of a ship—upside down.

Five miles after the tunnel was my first and only true climb of the day, a 1,000-foot ascent over seven miles, followed by a quick 1,700-foot descent. The wheel held up wonderfully. Nary a wobble. I felt good about the integrity of my bike, confident the trip would be completed with no further incidents. I was a machine, conditioned to move forward, only forward. My objective: Battle Mountain.

Aside from the Carlin Tunnel, there were only three other landmarks worth mentioning between Elko and Battle Mountain:

- The Beowawe Westbound Rest Area
- Crossing over the Humboldt River
- A cluster of nine trees, perhaps whitebark pine, that interrupted the uninterruptable flat basin known as Nevada
- Oh… and a dust devil kicked up about forty-three miles into my ride.

It took only four hours to reach Battle Mountain. The genesis of its name was up for debate, but it was widely accepted that George Tannehill and twenty-three other settlers battled against the Native Americans for the mountain. Kind of like naming a town that had flooded, Flood City, but who was I to comment, having named no towns myself?

After the exit, I arrived at the Owl Club, which offered *Family Dining*. Next to that was the defunct Nevada Hotel, boasting *Fun - Food - Casino - Family*. Next to that was the Owl Motel: *Queen Size Beds - Air conditioned - Phones*. The price of $34.95 was painted on the side of the west exterior wall, twenty feet high.

With all these offerings, out here in the middle of the Nevada desert, I had everything I needed.

I loved casinos. I loved them more when I won. If you were at a good casino, just standing by the craps table would get you free booze, and that was something to celebrate. It was an adrenaline rush, watching with anticipation as the dealer flipped over that last card; following the wheel as it came to a slow stop and the ball bounced into its final position; or cheering as the dice landed, hopefully without adding up to seven.

After checking into the Owl Motel, I headed to the casino. The casino was dark, small, and smelled of cigarette smoke. Every attempt to keep the daylight out was made by covering the front windows with blackout tint. I believed it was the same sort of tint Wilfredo used in his car back in Nebraska.

One guy was sitting at the slot machines. He didn't appear to notice me when I entered the room. Another guy sat at the blackjack table and seemed annoyed with me for letting sunlight creep in when I opened the door. The woman behind the bar was trying to recapture her youth through aggressive makeup application.

It was early and shots of Jim Beam were only $2.50. I ordered a double—a four-fingered pour. It was going to either be a long night or a short morning.

This was truly a very sad place, but I took great joy in my first double shot of Beam. I ordered another, along with the "New York Steak." According to the menu, it was the *BEST CUT YOU CAN BUY!*

The steak wasn't too bad, but I was pretty buzzed when the food arrived. Working through my second double, I walked over to the blackjack table.

I threw down twenty dollars and quickly doubled my money. This single action both paid for my dinner and whiskey and damn near caused a fight to break out between me and the unhappy man at the table, who was now even unhappier than he was before I let the light in.

"You sum bitch! You done took my cards!" He slammed his hand on the table.

"Now Sam, let's just calm down," the dealer intervened.

"Took your cards!? I didn't TOOK nothing! The dealer DEALT me the cards!" Whiskey made me courageous.

"You best walk away son 'fore I kick your ass out of this town!" Sam scowled.

The bartender called me over and offered to comp me on my third shot, which I took to my room—the worst I had ever paid for. I'd been in jail cells with more personality. The TV was chained to the dresser, which was screwed to the wall. Its minimal selection of channels offered little entertainment. The towels were stained; the pillow had no structure; and God only knew what sort of biology was living in the carpet.

I sat on the bed. Suddenly, I felt empty, knowing that in a few days the trip would be over. I had no idea what my future had in store anymore. No longer the same person I was when I left, I had no desire to go back to that life. I didn't want to go back to any of it. My job, my house… I wanted to get to Truckee, go to the wedding, and then disappear.

Now did I turn in for the night or go back down to the casino, get another whiskey, and antagonize Sam at the blackjack table?

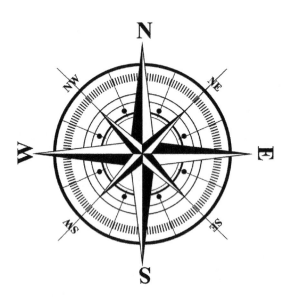

CHAPTER 21

DAY THIRTY-ONE

SEPTEMBER 21, 2001

Today's Ride: Battle Mountain, Nevada - Winnemucca, Nevada
Today's Distance: 70 Miles

The curtains in my room successfully kept the neon light out during the night and the sunlight out, come morning.

When I woke up to pee, it didn't occur to me to look at the clock. I scratched my ass and yawned on the way to the bathroom.

Outside the casino the night before, I had come across a flyer for the 2001 World Human Powered Speed Challenge, to be held right here in Battle Mountain, Nevada, Oct 1–6, 2001. I wondered if I should stay and watch. After all, I'd cycled across the Great Plains, over the Rocky Mountains, and across the Great Salt Lake Desert. I could even be a contender.

The year before, Sam Whittingham broke the record by going 82.819 miles per hour over two hundred meters on a customized recumbent[52] bicycle wrapped in an aerodynamic shell. The spectacular event also managed to combine both the imperial and metric

52 A bicycle design that places the rider in a laid-back reclining position.

systems, in this case miles per hour over meters—only in the good ol' U.S. of A.

Though, I didn't think I could handle spending ten more days in Battle Mountain, for any reason. Maybe Sam and I would become buddies in the end, or maybe he'd end up shooting me.

Battle Mountain was an armpit. In fact, in 2001, *Washington Post Magazine* deemed it the "Armpit of America." It was awarded this name due to its "… lack of character and charm… this pathetic assemblage of ghastly buildings and nasty people…"

Upon receiving this title, Battle Mountain made lemonades out of lemons and convinced Old Spice to sponsor an annual event— Festival in the Pit.

I lifted up the back end of my bike and spun the rear wheel. It was perfectly true; all the spokes were taut. By all appearances, it was holding up nicely. The tyre pressure was good. I had no need to add air. I strapped on my pack and headed out for breakfast at the Owl Restaurant, after which I continued westward on I-80.

With only fifty-four miles slated for the day, I was in a bigger hurry to leave Battle Mountain than I was to arrive in Winnemucca. In lieu of participating in the 2001 World Human Powered Speed Challenge, I decided to turn my ride to Winnemucca into the 2001 World Human Powered Casual Challenge. At sixteen miles per hour, I would cross the finish line in about three and a half hours. I didn't even bother taking any food, just two bottles of water.

Overlooking the old California Emigrant Trail, I passed the empty town of Valmy, named after the Battle of Valmy, fought during the French Revolution in 1792. All these empty towns were a vision of the past, holding onto life however they could. A dot on a map.

I came across a family fixing a flat tyre on their 1980s Pontiac station wagon.

Two kids were in the back, bouncing around, misbehaving, as good children should do when stuck in the back of a station wagon in ninety-degree heat, sans seat belts. The father was on both knees, working hard to loosen the rusted lug nuts on the left front wheel. The mother held a baby and stood behind her husband, actually *in* the right lane of I-80. They had chosen not to take full advantage of the handsome shoulder available. It was only a matter of time before the husband was taken out by a distracted driver.

I stopped, pulled out one of my water bottles, and took a swig. With a smile, I asked, "Do you guys need some help?"

They clearly didn't see me coming because my arrival scared the shit out of the couple. The woman, giving me a very stern look, moved around to the front of the car. From there, she looked me up and down.

Who is she to judge me? I thought. *It is me, her hero, a salty, sweaty, smelly beacon of hope, a messenger from God, sent to fix their flat. This charitable event means I am destined for sainthood.*

The father, perhaps fearing I was an undercover ICE agent, responded with a bit of hesitation in his voice. "No, we are fine," he said slowly with a Hispanic accent.

My help was not wanted—sainthood was put on hold. I replaced my water bottle and rode away toward Winnemucca.

Did I appear dangerous? Was there a serial killer on the loose in Nevada riding a bicycle that I should have been aware of?

An action selfie shot.

A few miles further a deer lay bloated in the middle of the shoulder. Its legs aimed at the clouds and tongue dangled out. A piece of plastic from the front end of the vehicle that hit it lay three feet away along with a bunch of little shiny plastic pieces, the remnants of a headlamp. The first wave of visitors had already arrived—the flies, laying their larvae. Vultures circled above. The smell was noticeable, but not yet overbearing.

Nevada Department of Wildlife would charge you with poaching if you tried to eat roadkill, but of these fifty United States, thirty allowed you to cook up whatever critter you found lying on the roadside. As a matter of fact, a cottage industry of roadkill cookbooks was available.

The Totalled RoadKill Cookbook

Quick-Fix Cooking with Roadkill

The Original Road Kill Cookbook

Route 66 Roadkill Recipes Binder

It was estimated that autos in the United States killed over four hundred million animals a year. One hundred million were killed in research. Statistically speaking, if you were an animal, you would have a better chance of survival in a research lab than you would running around the United States wild and free.

The sun beat down. I pressed on and soon found myself taking Exit 178, a mile-long exit ramp that led to Winnemucca Boulevard and straight to the Frontier Motel. The motel offered both daily and weekly rates and—best of all—a pool, which was situated right smack in the middle of the parking lot.

Two days and 101 years earlier, at the intersection of Bridge and Fourth, it was said that Butch Cassidy and the Sundance Kid, along with their gang the Wild Bunch, robbed the First National Bank of Winnemucca. They got off with over thirty-two thousand dollars in gold, and nary a person was injured, hurt, or killed. Winnemucca, deciding to turn this black eye into a badge of honor, now celebrated Butch Cassidy Days.

Celebrating criminals such as Butch and the Sundance Kid wasn't unusual. Northfield, Minnesota, celebrated Defeat of Jesse James Day, complete with a shootout reenactment of James and his gang robbing the First National Bank in Northfield. A bit misleading, as both Jesse and Frank James escaped. Jesse survived another eight years, until one day his friend Robert Ford thanked him for adjusting a crooked picture by putting a bullet in the back of his head.

The difference between Jesse James Day in Northfield and Butch Cassidy Days in Winnemucca was Jesse James actually did carry out the robbery. Turned out, Butch Cassidy was six hundred miles away in Tipton, Wyoming, at the time of the Winnemucca job, robbing a train. So, although the plaque on the Winnemucca bank tells us Butch Cassidy robbed the place, he did so only in spirit.

I checked into the Frontier Motel and turned on the AC, moving the dial all the way to blue. Even with my brief pit stop, I made it in just under four hours.

Grabbing the Winnemucca phonebook found in the nightstand, I searched for Chinese restaurants, deciding on Wonderful House because of its name. Despite the fact that Winnemucca had one of the largest Chinatowns in Nevada in the 1890s, its Chinese restaurant options were slim pickings these days.

Over eleven thousand Chinese people worked on the Transcontinental Railroad, which was completed in 1869. They were the most instrumental group of laborers on the team. They were also the most abused and underpaid group, assigned the most dangerous jobs, which took an estimated two thousand lives. Eventually, they went on strike. The only thing they got from it was better treatment; their pay remained half that of other groups.

The government, adding salt to the wound, rewarded the Chinese laborers with the Page Act of 1875, which prohibited Chinese women from entering the United States, marking an end to open borders. In 1882, seven years after the Page Act, the Chinese Exclusion Act banned all Chinese men from immigrating to the United States.

It wouldn't be until 1943, sixty-one years later, that the Magnuson Act (Chinese Exclusion Repeal Act) was adopted. Had it not been for the Magnuson Act, I'd probably be eating a burrito for dinner. So, thank you, Warren G. Magnuson.

Returning to the motel, I avoided the pool and settled into my bed.

My bike leaned against the wall; my cycling attire soaked in the sink; and the TV attempted to hold my attention. I was bored in a cheap motel in the desert and too lazy to do anything about it.

It was late afternoon. I thought about getting a six pack of beer.

I should get a six pack of beer, I told myself. *Yeah, but then I'd have to get up, put on my shoes, walk outside a few hundred yards to the gas station, find the brand of beer I like, look at the chips, find the bag of chips I like, decide if I want salsa or not, and if do want salsa, figure out what I'm gonna use as a bowl. After all that decision making, I'll have to pay for it and walk all the way back to my room.*

It all seemed like way too much work.

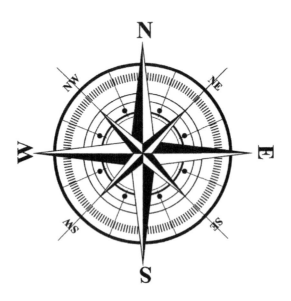

CHAPTER 22

DAY THIRTY-TWO

SEPTEMBER 22, 2001

Today's Ride: Winnemucca, Nevada - Lovelock, Nevada
Today's Distance: 72 Miles

May 15, 1918, Lieutenant George Boyle had less than sixty hours of flight time when he climbed into his Curtiss Jenny airplane. The plan: fly from Washington, DC, to Philadelphia to deliver 124 pounds of airmail. Instead he got lost, ran low on gas, and crashed in Maryland.

Lucky for Lieutenant Boyle, his fiancé's dad oversaw the new airmail service and gave him another chance.

This time, he was given overwhelmingly simple instructions: follow the Chesapeake Bay towards Philadelphia. And yet, he ran out of gas and crashed again.

Lieutenant Boyle never flew for the airmail service again, but this did not deter the airmail service from expanding all the way to California, doing so with an innovative idea.

In 1920, without navigational charts, radar, or radio—and with the potential of another Lieutenant Boyle always looming— hundreds if not thousands of large concrete arrows along with

beacon towers were placed every ten miles, across the entire country, to guide pilots. It was called the Transcontinental Airway, and in
Winnemucca, Beacon 32 still stood in full operation.

The whole system went extinct with the advent of radio and
radar, then almost disappeared entirely when WWII started. Most
of the arrows and towers were destroyed to avoid pointing the
Japanese in the right direction if they ever made it to the mainland.

To think that in 1860, we had the Pony Express. Sixty summers
later, we created a lighted path for airplane mailmen, and only 49
summers after that, we landed a man on the moon. In 109 summers,
we went from delivering the mail by horse to space travel.

But me, I opted for a bicycle, the purest form of transportation.
The bicycle evolved from the 1817 invention called the dandy
horse—which had no chain, brakes, or pedals, basically an adult
version of a kids Strider. The French, in the 1860s, would coin the
word bicycle when pedals were attached to the front wheel. The
penny-farthing entered the scene in 1870 and gave rise to bike clubs
and bike racing. The French would eventually develop the derailleur
in the 1900s, which allowed for bikes to have gears, after ten decades
of improved designs and engineering.

Just before Lovelock, I came across another vehicle with a flat
tyre. The driver was struggling to pull the spare from her trunk.

"Would you like some help?" I had already dismounted my bike
and laid it on the ground.

"Why yes," she said. "That would be wonderful. Say, I saw you
bicycling a while back. Aren't you hot?"

"Hot?" I laughed. "I'm fried. Been biking for…" I had to think for a second, seemed like I had been biking for two years. "… for a couple of weeks, I think."

I pulled out the tyre and rummaged around the trunk looking for the jack. Everything was probably exactly where it was when the car rolled off the showroom floor ten years ago.

"Are you headed to San Francisco?"

"I suppose I am, though my next stop is Truckee to go to a wedding. Then I'll continue on to San Fran."

"My daughter just moved to San Francisco, and I'm sure it would be okay if you wanted to stay with her for a few days. Here is her name and number. I'll call her and let her know you'll be there in a couple of weeks."

I was sure the offer was made with true sincerity. Still, the idea that a mom would offer an invitation to a complete stranger—a really dirty, stinky stranger, riding a bicycle across the desert—to stay with her daughter, simply because he changed her flat tyre—I found odd.

"I'm heading to Lovelock," she said. "It's just twenty miles. Would you like a ride? We can put your bike in the back. I'm sure it would fit." She opened the back door and moved some stuff around. "Oh sure, look. There is plenty of room."

"No, but thank you."

I arrived at Lovelock in a little over an hour.

I took Exit 107 and came across the Royal Inn, which offered "courtyard suites." The courtyard, from what I could tell, was a bituminous parking lot, and the suite was just a room like any other.

The room was actually pretty nice. The AC had been left on low, so I flipped it to high and stripped out of my cycling outfit. Looking at my naked self in the mirror, the difference between my white and tanned bits was painfully obvious.

Across the street was the C Punch Casino, so without bothering to shower, I got dressed and headed straight there. All I wanted to do was spend the next hour enjoying some water, a few beers, a couple of appetizers, and dinner—preferably in the form of a massive chunk of meat.

I'm sorry reader, it's Nevada. Are you still entertained? Sometimes the days just end. You arrive to your destination and can't remember how you got there or what happened along the way. I know these ramblings are not those of a writer. A writer should be able to penetrate the blank canvas and describe it in great detail.

Your whole being goes into some sort of autopilot. You disappear in your mind, you dream, and suddenly you have 30-40-50 miles behind you. You don't remember crossing that bridge or avoiding an auto part or dead body. So, I ask you to hang in there, we are almost there. Just 125 more miles and three chapters to go.

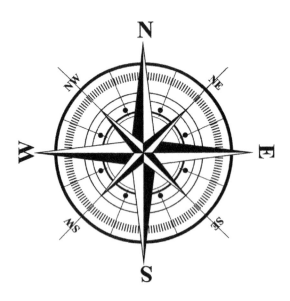

CHAPTER 23

DAY THIRTY-THREE

SEPTEMBER 23, 2001

Today's Ride: Lovelock, Nevada - Reno, Nevada
Today's Distance: 93 Miles

> "Watch carefully, because everything happens fast. The chase. The desert. The shack. The girl. The roadblock. The end."
>
> —*Vanishing Point*

When I left Wendover, I started to realize my journey was coming to an end. I suppose it sounds odd that it took me until crossing the border of Nevada to notice that I was nearing my destination. Perhaps that was why I had spent an extra day at the Red Garter. It certainly wasn't the buffet that kept me there.

I had decided to stay another night in an attempt to push the finish line back one more day, knowing California was just a few days away. In a couple of weeks, I'd trade my Lycra shorts in for a pair of pleated dockers.

No longer was I the person I was less than a month before. The first few days of the trip, I was depressed because I had entered self-imposed isolation. Now, my depression was because I would soon reenter society. I suppose I'd been looking for a way in while seeking a way out.

I suppose I never left society; I left the idea of what society expected of me. Weeks ago, I wanted for all this to be over. Now, I wished Truckee was four years away.

What was next for your hero? Sitting behind a desk for twelve hours a day? Spending weekends keeping my yard tidy, catching up on laundry? Thursday nights watching water-cooler TV with my friends? Pretending to like my neighbors so I could borrow a power tool when needed? I was afraid I would return and become that reflection I left back at Crawford's Bar & Grill in Sioux Falls.

The road freed me from the daily chaos and doldrums of life. It freed me from everything. I had spent the last few weeks recreating who I was, without knowing it was happening. I realized now I could be anywhere and anyone or nowhere and no one.

Ride, eat, drink, sleep. Selfish? Perhaps. I had given the world nothing over the past few weeks that could be considered a benefit to the greater good. Nor was I taking from it, aside from temporary space. I suppose I gave back a little. I was keeping Subway in business and providing jobs for those I purchased drinks and shelter from. Perhaps I inspired someone I spoke with along the way. Or maybe someone I didn't speak with, someone who saw me riding along a desert highway and thought, *man, I need to do that.*

I was drifting, not in search of anything or running away from anything. At least, not that I was aware of, anyway.

Despite all of those thoughts racing around my mind, I was still excited to arrive in Reno. I felt like celebrating, if for no other reason than to be done with riding across the vast Great Basin known as Nevada.

Reno offered lights, excitement, and casinos. Reno was my Champs-Élysées. I was convinced people were there waiting for me with champagne hand-ups. Lining the streets to celebrate my arrival.

I was still more than five hours away, but the mayor of Reno—I was sure—was busy preparing the town and warming up the band to celebrate my victorious arrival. Would there be ticker tape? Perhaps, but it wasn't necessary. I was but a simple man.

I'd enter town, popping a wheelie across the finish line. Or better yet, under the Reno Arch, which famously read: *Reno, The Biggest Little City in the World.*

That was going to be my Arc de Triomphe.

I stopped, dismounted, and stretched eighteen miles outside of Lovelock. Grabbing my bike, I walked into the desert, set up my camera, and laid down in the sand to take a selfie. I was bored and had time to kill. I wanted to give the mayor of Reno plenty of time to set up my celebration.

It was eerily quiet, even traffic was next to nil. Perhaps as a moment of silence for the massive graveyard I was crossing.

This stretch of desert was known as the Forty Mile Desert to the emigrants and was the deadliest section of the California Trail. With their "prairie schooner" in tow, it took an average of two days to cross. Because of the heat and lack of drinkable water, over ten thousand animals perished and 953 emigrants died trying to cross this section alone. Mark Twain wrote after traveling the route, "It was a dreary pull and a long and thirsty one, for we had no water. From one extremity of this desert to the other, the road was white with the bones of oxen and horses. It would hardly be an exaggeration to say that we could have walked the forty miles and set our feet on a bone at every step!"

With a selfie documented on the roll of 35mm film, I gathered my bike and continued.

I passed through Fernley. The Love's truck stop offered a short break, where I bought a couple of sandwiches and a Gatorade for lunch. Totally unsatisfying, but it was enough to get me the rest of the way to Reno.

Two miles after Fernley, I crossed the Truckee River, which filled the mysterious Pyramid Lake, twenty-three miles north.

Pyramid Lake, with its pyramid-shaped limestone features, was twenty-nine miles long, eight miles wide, 350 feet deep, and home to the ancient legend of the water babies.

Until John Frémont came across them in 1844, the peaceful Paiute tribe lived here in seclusion. To keep the tribe strong and healthy to grow and prosper, the Paiute took babies which were born weak or deformed and threw them into the dark waters of the lake.

Many claimed they heard the crying of those Paiute babies coming from the deep, dark waters of the lake. The legend had the making of a great Art Bell episode.

The first sign of Reno was an off-ramp to nowhere, placed in anticipation of some inevitable future sprawl. Then, there were the outskirts, followed by an outlet mall and fast food restaurants. Next, midcentury restaurants and motels littered what was formerly the outskirts of Reno, followed by the suburbs. Behind the hills rose a tightly knit conclave of hotels and casinos crammed into one location. Somewhere in that concrete and glass was the Reno Arch.

Instead of the crowds of people I imagined waiting for me downtown, I was promptly hit up by a panhandler. I offered him a few dollars in exchange for taking my picture under the arch.

Downtown, a motorcycle rally had merged with a tattoo expo, filling the streets with leather chaps, bandanas, a marginally acceptable cover band, and thousands of Harleys. The guttural sound of exhaust pipes echoed off the buildings; leather vests claimed loyalty to motorcycle clubs; and I saw enough tattoos to cover the walls of the Louvre.

I strolled by, wearing my Lycra bike shorts, dirty red shirt, and red bandana, pushing my little bicycle. I was the one drawing stares, the outcast of this group of outcasts.

A very large, mean-looking guy with a ponytail, braided beard, leather motorcycle vest loaded with patches, and a wallet chain dangling from his hip walked right up to me and stared me square in the eye. In a deep raspy voice, he said, "Looks like you brought the wrong bike," in a way that sounded like I should seriously consider leaving.

"I suppose I did," I said. "I just spent the past couple of weeks biking from Minneapolis."

He looked at me, then my bike, then gave me a smile.

"So, do you think you could take my picture?" I asked, digging out my Olympus.

"Sure!"

He grabbed my camera, laughed, then snapped a photo.

"There is a tattoo expo going on," he said. "You should check it out."

"I don't have any place to stash my bike and pack."

"Look, a group of us are sitting over there. Leave it with us, we'll watch it for ya."

He pointed to a cluster of motorcycles by a pop-up, open-air canopy tent. Under it sat five guys and a couple of women, drinking beers. Two of the guys were watching our conversation. They nodded in the affirmative when I looked over.

"Sure!" I said. "That would be great."

I'd made it to Reno. Why the hell not?

The tattoo expo was buzzing—literally. Artists with open booths were scattered all over the place, inking their subjects. I spent a half-hour watching them collaborate with their canvasses. I even thought about getting a tattoo to commemorate my ride, but remembered how much I hated needles and returned to my bicycle.

"What do ya think?" the biker asked when I returned. "Going to get some ink?"

He handed me a beer.

"Nope, I hate needles."

"Wanna shot?" He handed me a half-empty bottle of Jack Daniels.

"Yes. Yes, I do." I took two big gulps. The men gave nods of approval.

I hung out with them for about fifteen minutes. Then I thanked them, and we hugged it out in traditional male fashion—the one-hand-clasp pull-in, followed by two pats to the back.

"Be safe, brother!" the bikers called out.

I raised my hand, gave them the peace sign, then turned the corner.

I made my way to the Truckee River and rode along Riverside Drive then jumped on Fourth Street, where I found the Old Forty West Motel. It offered kitchenettes and weekly and monthly rates, none of which I needed.

Just down the street was the Flowing Tide Pub, an Irish-influenced sports bar that offered typical US American bar food. My celebratory meal in Reno, which I had envisioned I would be having with hundreds of star-struck fans at the finest steakhouse in town, ended up with just me, on the outskirts of town, alone at a bar. I ordered mozzarella sticks, a blue cheese bacon burger, and a couple of shots of Jack Daniels in honor of my new biker brothers.

"Califia, a Mythical Island Paradise"

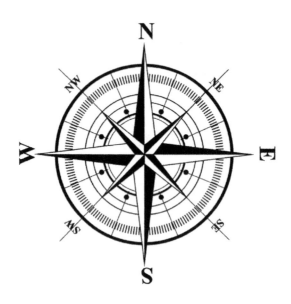

CHAPTER 24

DAY THIRTY-FOUR

SEPTEMBER 24, 2001

Today's Ride: Reno, Nevada - Truckee, California
Today's Distance: 32 Miles

Thirty-two miles and three thousand feet of elevation gain to Truckee.

Just a quick "Zip-a-Dee-Doo-Dah" to the top.

My last day. It felt like I had left Minneapolis yesterday. But here I was at the base of the Sierra Nevadas. I would be in Truckee for lunch.

Instinctively, I opted to continue riding along the shoulder of I-80. I didn't even bother to look at the map to see if there was perhaps another squiggly line that would take me to the Celestial City. No, by this time, I knew all there was to know about America's highways, byways, backroads, squiggly lines, bridges, and waterways. I knew the different types of asphalts. There was quiet asphalt, perpetual pavement, warm-mix asphalt, thin asphalt overlay, and porous asphalt. Each had its own unique look, texture, and longevity.

Besides, looking back, I couldn't think of a single time I made a bad decision on this trip. My execution had been as precise as a wrecking ball.

It was just a straight shot, after all. I made no attempt to discredit my plan by asking a local if biking I-80 to Truckee was safe, or even legal.

The first twelve miles had the makings of an excellent ride. The shoulder was robust, smooth, clear of debris, and made of warm-mix asphalt. A gentle tailwind pushed me west toward the Golden State—my land of milk and honey.

I soon reached the California border. Fetching my camera, I took the obligatory photo of my bike leaning against the sign.

Welcome to California - SIERRA COUNTY LINE

The sign contained an image of an *Eschscholzia californica*—aka, the California poppy.

I did it. I had made it to California. In just three, maybe four hours of grinding up the Sierra Nevadas, I would be in Truckee.

The minute I crossed the border into California, the comfortable shoulder changed to multiple variations of concrete and bituminous. The shoulder narrowed, and with that, a barrage of semi-trucks and massive SUVs filled the highway. They seemed to appear out of nowhere.

The skies turned dark grey as I entered the valley of the shadow of death. Before me, a treacherous land filled with dragons, goblins, and beasts from the mouth of hell. They lurked under the six bridges, in the hollers, and on the countless variations of concrete and asphalt I was forced to travel across.

Nine miles into California, I hit some debris and heard a *ping* sound. The all-too-familiar wobble returned. I had broken another spoke on the rear wheel. The spoke dangled and scraped the frame at every rotation.

I jumped off my bike and removed the broken spoke with the speed of a NASCAR pit crew. I reached back, released the rear brake, and pressed on. This wasn't my first rodeo, spoke.

Eleven miles to go.

Wobbling two more miles, I hit a chunk of shredded tyre. Another *ping* that echoed into the valley, alerting the goblins of my presence. I didn't stop. I had started with thirty-six spokes, but now

I was down to thirty-four. Theoretically, I could break three and a half spokes per mile and still make it to town.

The road became bumpy, and there seemed to be an increase of debris—obviously the work of the goblins. All it would take was one large rock or crack in the road to finally destroy what was left of the rear wheel.

Miles passed, and I successfully stayed upright.

Eight miles left.

Seven miles.

Six miles.

Just five miles out, I approached the sixth and final crossing of the Truckee River. The bridge was narrow and appeared to be more than two hundred feet long, if I was to guess. It might as well have been ten miles.

The bridge offered nothing in the way of a shoulder, just a narrow, unprotected passage. It offered a misleading sense of safety as I crossed the Truckee River one last time before reaching the town of the same name.

Behind me, the road curved around the bend and hid behind the trees. As far as I could see, I had a green light to cross.

As birds chirped and the wind gently worked its way through the trees, I heard the calm babble of the river below. It was then that the distant rumble of two diesel engines entered the arena. I was halfway across the bridge when I looked back and saw the two semi-trucks spewing black exhaust, rolling side by side.

My heart sank as I looked over the bridge for a possible escape route. I didn't have the nerve to leap fifty feet into the shallow river.

With everything I had, I increased my cadence in hopes of speeding up my crossing. The trucks closed in at a greater pace.

Close now, I could see the end of the bridge, maybe twenty feet ahead. Pedaling with everything I had, my bike wobbled relentlessly, slowing down my pace. The trucks had arrived at the bridge. Each fired off a long belch on their horns. With just ten feet to go, two metal drainage grates stopped me from pedaling on. Without a thought, I jumped off my bike and ran as fast as I could that last ten feet, with my bike in tow.

Just as I cleared the bridge, the semis caught me. I threw my bike and dove over the metal barrier, tumbling down the dirt embankment.

I lay on my back, taking refuge in the Land of Beulah.[53] Every one of my sunburned, bloodied, and bruised limbs outstretched among the weeds, dirt, and discarded trash.

I breathed and stared above past the clouds and the blue sky. I traveled deep into the darkness of space. Life's whole damn circle in the span of a few feet. My Star Child stared back at me from the cosmos.

Perhaps taking I-80 wasn't such a smart idea after all.

It took twenty minutes for me to get my nerve back. I could see the tops of more semi-trucks rumbling past above me. It was five more miles to Truckee.

Grabbing my bike, I dragged the stubborn mule up the embankment. Back on the highway, I proceeded west and exited a few miles later, coasting into downtown Truckee.

---

53 The peaceful land where the pilgrim awaits the call to the Celestial City.

Truckee was brimming with outdoor outfitters, coffee shops, and overpriced tourist traps. It took little effort to find a bike shop. Walking into the shop, I removed my pack and dropped it on the ground, then limped my bike to the service counter in hopes of finding someone who could fix my rear wheel. My wounds from I-80 were now dry and flakey. I must have been a sorry sight.

Even so, the service guy couldn't be bothered. He watched my feeble approach to the counter, and it still took him far too long to even ask if he could help me.

"Yeah?" was all he could muster.

"I'm biking cross-country, and I broke a couple of spokes. Any chance you have time today?"

He looked at the rear wheel, then back at me. He didn't say a word.

"I know, I know. I need a new rear wheel, but I've made it two thousand miles. I just need it to hold on a little longer. It doesn't need to be pretty; it just needs to be true and to live for another week."

He looked between my rear wheel, me, and the bike he was wrenching on.

"Yeah, okay. I can get to it in about forty-five minutes. Leave it here, but you need a new wheel."

One and a half hours later, I was rolling true again in search of my rebound's sister's place.

Turns out she lived in a cabin, my House Beautiful[54] for the next week.

---

54 In *The Pilgrim's Progress*, the palace, which sits atop the Hill of Difficulty and serves as a rest stop for pilgrims to the Celestial City.

I knocked a couple of times at the front door with no answer. I heard voices around back, so I ventured around the side of the house. Four people sat, having beers and talking. When I showed up, a blonde woman looked up at me.

"Are you Stacy?" I asked.

"Cory?"

"Yep."

"We've been waiting for you!"

Everyone stood up, all smiles. I didn't expect anyone to be waiting for me. Maybe they had missed my celebratory arrival into Reno yesterday.

"I can't believe it! We've been waiting all day. We have a bunch of people coming over to celebrate your arrival. Would you like a beer?"

I smiled and hobbled over to the stairs leading to the deck.

"Yes," I said, as honestly as I'd ever said anything in my life. "Yes, I would like a beer."

The blonde looked at me more closely.

"A shower," she said. "Do you want to take a shower?"

"Yes, yes. I would like to shower. A beer and a shower."

Bathed and beered, I joined the festivities.

"So," one of the guests asked, "how did you get here from Reno?"

"I took I-80."

"You took I-80?!"

The group looked amazed.

"That's so dangerous."

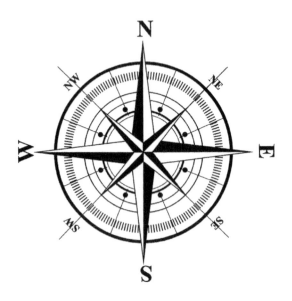

AFTERWORD

"Now this is not the end. It is not even the beginning of the end.
But it is, perhaps, the end of the beginning."
—WINSTON CHURCHILL

The Wedding

Although things didn't turn out well for your hero and the rebound, it worked out in the long run. When we finally reconnected, I would say I was pretty excited to see her. However, her feelings were clearly not the same as she informed me that we had already broken up. A bit surprised but not devastated, I responded, "Really? Because I've been biking... alone... for a few weeks. I'm pretty sure that would have been a conversation I would have remembered?!"

My time in Truckee was still great. Before rebound arrived, I had the opportunity to become friends with and hang out with the Truckee gang (friends of rebound's sister). It was a fantastic time, hiking the Sierra Nevadas, kayaking around Lake Tahoe, and enjoying a challenging, yet humbling seventy-two-mile road ride with a few of the guys who schooled me on speed and intensity. I was a footman trying to keep up with horses. My Olympic trials were put on hold.

The leaves were changing; salmon were heading back up Taylor Creek to spawn; and I was officially single again. I debated moving into Calvin's Airstream—he was looking for a roommate—and finding a job at Heavenly Ski Resort as a lift operator. I had formed a small crush on one of the women in the group but never acted on it. I was sure had I stayed, we would have become an "item," at least for a short time. To quote my new buddy Calvin, "You don't date in Truckee, you just get your turn."

After what I would have to say was one of the best weddings I had ever had the pleasure to be a part of, I returned to the cabin and packed up my gear. The gang bought me a new cycling helmet as a gift. They made it clear how upset they were I was riding without one. I had to promise to always wear one when cycling moving forward. Pinky swear.

Newly-acquired helmet just in time for the wedding

Grass Valley – Cousin Amy

The next morning, I left early to avoid goodbyes. I was not a fan of goodbyes. When we moved from Burnsville, MN, to Scottsdale, AZ, I remember wanting to say goodbye to all my friends but that wasn't part of Dad's plan. His plan was no goodbyes. Just get in the car and go. I was six. When we moved back to Minnesota from Scottsdale, it was the same thing. Around 4:00 a.m., with the Suburban loaded up, Dad woke me up and said, "Let's go, you're driving the first leg to Tucumcari." I was seventeen. He must not like goodbyes either.

I opted to stay off I-80 and headed thirty-nine miles north on CA-89, which offered no shoulder but a nice descent most of the way to Sierraville. I stopped for breakfast at Smithneck Farms Café. From there, I called my cousin Amy in Grass Valley, CA, and told her I was passing through on my way to San Francisco on my bike, heading out on CA-49.

Grass Valley was a windy eighty-one miles west with 5,098 feet of elevation gain and no shoulder.

Lucky for me, Amy took that call to mean, "Pick me up." I ran into her at Sierra City, CA, cutting out the remaining fifty-nine miles left to Grass Valley.

She did a U-turn on CA-49. Laughing, she yelled out of her truck, "HEY CORY, WHAT ARE YOU DOING?!"

"I don't know. I guess I decided to bike to California."

We hugged then loaded the bike and gear in the back of her SUV.

"Oh my God, Cory. I can't believe you biked all the way out here. Did you have lunch at Smithneck's in Sierraville? Oh my God, their food is sooooo goooood."

In general, Amy's mind traveled at a speed of about 185 mph. She got it from her mom, my aunt Mary, who was the same way. Like sharks, they didn't sleep but were required to keep moving. I recalled watching Aunt Mary doing squats while washing dishes at Grandma's one Christmas.

After we caught up and I'd given her a brief overview of the trip, I mentioned to her that I wasn't really happy with the direction my life was going, nor was I that unhappy. I was… dissatisfied. There was more out there. I had tasted it, but I had never dived in. Always, I felt I had to be the responsible oldest son, the reliable older brother. I'm not sure I was either, but I was sure I could still be those things no matter where I was or what I was doing. Truth was I stopped me from being me. I trapped myself in an environment that wasn't designed for me.

"How old are you now?" she asked.

"Thirty-one."

"That's it, you're having your Saturn's Return."

"My what?"

"Your Saturn's Return. It's when Saturn returns to the place it was when you were born and creates a strong urge for change. You can either listen to this or ignore it. Most people ignore it."

She was excited to share this philosophy with me, so she continued. "You said you don't really know why, but you had this urge to remove yourself from your current situation. This is it. You are listening. You are accepting change! I love it!"

Amy had an old house she was fixing up which had a couch she offered me to sleep on for as long as I wanted, a live-in boyfriend, and a ghost she called Nancy.

"I keep a sheet over the TV because Nancy likes to turn it on in the middle of the night. When it's covered, she leaves it off."

Who was Nancy, you ask? She was an old woman who died in the house but still had opinions about how things should be done. For example, Amy placed four swatch colors on the wainscot in the living room in an effort to decide which color to choose. Every morning, she would wake up and all the swatches were on the ground except one, "Summer Lemonade Yellow."

This happened five nights in a row. Apparently, Nancy had decided on "Summer Lemonade Yellow."

Amy wanted to build a fence around the house, I was eager to get my hands dirty. We dug holes, mixed concrete, erected the posts, and quickly filled them in with 2x4's and siding. The project wrapped up in a few days.

Staring at our accomplishment, beer in hand, Amy elbowed me in the rib and asked, "Are you tired of biking? If not, I've always wanted to bike the Oregon coast. We can call Becky (Amy's sister, my cousin), meet in Chico, and drive up. Take turns biking."

Amy, me, and peeps after building the fence in the background.

The Oregon Coast

We met Becky in Chico and then drove up to Florence, Oregon.

Becky's boyfriend decided he'd drive support the whole time, so he could work while we biked from Florence, Oregon, to Crescent City, California.

It was a total distance of 184 miles along the Pacific Coast Highway over four days. We only needed to do an average of 46 miles a day without gear, so each day was approached with very little sense of urgency. Additionally, we had a support vehicle if things took a turn for the worse.

Becky and me running the sand dunes in Oregon

We camped along the way, found a coffee shop in the morning somewhere, and sat for thirty to forty-five minutes talking. Then we'd ride, not always together. If we separated, whoever was out front would stop every once in a while to make sure everyone was good.

Night two was when I realized that Amy could sleep through anything. Two raccoons in full mortal combat with each other woke me up. They were only two feet from her head as she slept under the stars. I didn't know whether to wake her up or just laugh.

If you've never heard raccoons fighting, it is by far the loudest event in nature, second to that of perhaps a glacier calving or a pig squealing while being caught by a predator.

We ended our journey with beer, pizza, and psychedelic bowling at Tsunami Lanes.

Amy returned to Grass Valley. Becky dropped me off in San Francisco. With two weeks left before I had to return to Minneapolis, the plan was to hang in San Francisco for a couple of days, then cycle down to Carmel Valley where Becky lived and wait out my time journaling before heading back to a life unwanted.

San Francisco

My first day at the Green Tortoise Hostel off Broadway in San Francisco, I met Chris, a dude from England who had just arrived in the states. It was around happy hour, so we decided to grab a beer at the Bamboo Hut across the street. There, we met three more from

England and a couple from Scotland. Turns out three of the Brits were in the Army. This was their last night before shipping off to the Middle East to fight in the "War on Terror."

That night, six Brits and one Yank ventured out and hit five of the seven strip clubs in a one-block radius on Broadway—Little Darlings, Condor Club, Garden of Eden, Roaring 20's, and Vixen Gentlemen's Club. Every club comped us everything after the three soldiers told the bouncer they were heading off to war.

Day two was an exercise in recovering from a hangover. I sat in the lounge of the hostel and met a handful of people from all over the world who were just roaming the planet on a budget. A German girl had been all throughout South and Central America, alone. An older guy, whose wife passed away, sold his house and was traveling around the United States by bus and train with just his suitcase and a camera. A couple, she from Australia, him from Iraq, had met somewhere along the way in Southeast Asia, formed a romance and a gallery of tattoos along their journey.

My few weeks was nothing compared to these modern-day adventurers. It was a world I was now ready for. I was in a different headspace entirely. I wasn't even thinking about returning to Minneapolis.

Minneapolis felt insignificant. My job was insignificant. My house, car, "stuff"... all insignificant. It was decades behind me, a lifetime ago.

Of course, it helped that I had some walking around money. At the rate I was spending it, I had enough to last me about three years. A lot could happen in three years. Of course, a lot could stay the same, if I let it.

Back in Minneapolis, everything would stay the same—my commute to work, my friends (all of them admittedly wonderful), my career, my routine. In three years, I'd be three years older. My 401(k) would have forty-five thousand dollars more in it. I might have run a few more marathons, my waistline might have grown a bit, my hairline receded, but otherwise, all the same.

There would be a new bar or restaurant to try. A friend might bring another friend I hadn't met to happy hour, and my circle of friends would widen by one. Perhaps a trip—Costa Rica, Guatemala, Lithuania—would temporarily satisfy my wanderlust, but it would be short-lived, limited, forgotten. I'd return and be slammed with calls, emails, and projects that never ended. The routine would wait for me.

On the road, no one asked anything of me. I was quiet—pedaling, coasting, looking, hearing, smelling, seeing. I picked and chose what was important. I had never before had such control over who I was or wasn't. There was a saying, "'Un-fuck yourself; Be the person you were before all that stuff dimmed your shine." It was time to begin the process of un-fucking myself.

I decided to walk down to Jack Kerouac Alley, just a block and half away and pick up a copy of *On the Road* at City Lights Bookstore. Seemed like a thing one should do. Read the Viking sagas in Iceland, read Hemingway in Paris, read Bernard Moitessier if you found yourself sailing around the world.

San Francisco—Read Kerouac.

I hadn't paid for the second night yet so decided to check out and head south toward Carmel Valley. From the hostel, I headed up Columbus Ave to the Hyde Street Pier and then worked my way over to and through the Presidio. I did a little wandering around back toward Haight-Ashbury and then west through the Japanese Tea Garden and Golden Gate Park, which dumped me out onto the Pacific Coast Highway. I was shooting for Santa Cruz but made a few wrong turns and decided to stay the night in Miramar at the Quality Inn—it was anything but exciting. I grabbed a burger and a few beers at a little rustic bar a few doors down called The Barn.

The next day, I had lunch in Santa Cruz at El Hermosa Mar on Beach Street and settled in for the night at the Best Western in Marina. The road from Marina to Carmel was hit or miss along the PCH, but it was a nice casual fourteen miles to Carmel. Becky lived in Carmel Valley which would add another thirteen miles.

Carmel

Becky told me she had a friend who needed a house sitter in Carmel Highlands. It was a pretty easy sell. The midcentury house up in the mountains overlooked the Pacific Ocean. An old Ducati Café Racer was in the living room.

My job? Just be there.

My mornings were spent writing, thinking, and drinking pressed coffee.

On the fourth day, I made a decision that would change the entire trajectory of my life. I called my employer.

"Mark, thank you for holding my position, but I think I'm going to jump as high as I can, let the world revolve underneath me, and see where I land."

And with that, my last paycheck was automatically deposited into my account. I was unemployed.

Becky came over my last night, and we enjoyed a couple of bottles of wine. She was excited about my decision and offered to store my bike for as long as I needed. The next morning, she picked me up around 10:00 a.m. We drove to Nepenthe in Big Sur. It seemed a fitting place.

Nepenthe: Drug of forgetfulness.

Becky drove north, and I walked out onto the west side of the Pacific Coast Highway. It wasn't long until a beat-up old 1980s Jeep Wagoneer rounded the corner and came to a stop. The three occupants—man, woman, and dog—welcomed me in. Together, we headed toward Mexico....

El camino nos condujo a México.

"Looking behind, I am filled with gratitude,
Looking forward, I am filled with vision,
Looking upwards I am filled with strength,
Looking within, I discover peace."

—QUERO APACHE PRAYER

ABOUT THE AUTHOR

CORY MORTENSEN has ridden his collection of bicycles over a million miles of asphalt, dirt, mud, and backroads. In addition to the cross-country journey detailed in this book, he has traveled to over fifty-five countries, cycled from Minneapolis to Colorado solo to raise money for children born with congenital heart defects. He's completed sixteen marathons on five continents, and survived three days of running with the bulls in Spain.

Cory is a certified Advanced PADI diver, and has enjoyed taking in life under the waves in locations all over the world. In 2003, he took time off from roaming, and accidentally started and built a company which he sold in 2013. That same year he married his best friend, explored the state of Texas for two years. The couple sold everything they owned, jumped on a plane to Ecuador and volunteered, trekked, and explored South America for sixteen months before returning to Phoenix, Arizona, where he works as a consultant and is soon to be a bestselling author.

The Buddha and the Bee is his first memoir. He shares how a two-month leave of absence redefined his life's trajectory of sitting behind a desk and his decision to break society's chains so he could live life on his terms.

Contact the author at cory@corymortensen.com

www.thebuddhaandthebee.com

www.corymortensen.com

Follow Cory on Facebook and Instagram.

"This guy is crazy, someone who you don't want planning a trip for you, but who you'd probably love to have beers with or read a book he wrote. He's a great storyteller, adding tons of asides and background info." —E.W. Bertram, Reviewer

CORY MORTENSEN

UNLOST

ROAMING THROUGH SOUTH AMERICA ON A SPONTANEOUS JOURNEY

From the author of *THE BUDDHA AND THE BEE*. The saga continues!

Unlost is Cory Mortensen's second memoir. He shares his adventures as he explores the people and places of South America from the Mexican border to Argentina and beyond to Antarctica.

Find Cory's first books at www.TheBuddhaAndTheBee.com
Available in paperback, hardcover with color photos, and ebook.

Printed in Great Britain
by Amazon

83373496R00202